W9-BZG-312

LIBERATION
SQUARE

LIBERATION SQUARE

Inside the
Egyptian Revolution
and the Rebirth
of a Nation

ASHRAF KHALIL

St. Martin's Press ≋ New York

LIBERATION SQUARE. Copyright © 2011 by Ashraf Khalil. All rights reserved. Printed in the United States of America. For information, address St. Martin's Press, 175 Fifth Avenue, New York, N.Y. 10010.

www.stmartins.com

Design by Anna Gorovoy

Photo on title page by Ashraf Khalil

Library of Congress Cataloging-in-Publication Data

Khalil, Ashraf.
    Liberation Square : inside the Egyptian revolution and the rebirth of a nation / Ashraf Khalil. — 1st ed.
        p. cm.
    ISBN 978-1-250-00669-1 (hardcover)
    ISBN 978-1-4299-6244-5 (e-book)
    1. Egypt—History—Revolution, 2011.   2. Egypt—Politics and government—21st century.   I. Title.
    DT107.87.K43 2012
    962.05'5—dc23

                                                        2011038194

First Edition: January 2012

10 9 8 7 6 5 4 3 2 1

NEW HANOVER COUNTY
PUBLIC LIBRARY
201 CHESTNUT STREET
WILMINGTON, NC 28401

This book is dedicated to my mother, Hoda Ibrahim Aboleneen, who should have lived long enough to read it.

CONTENTS

CONTENTS

ACKNOWLEDGMENTS

This book never could have been written without the direct and indirect assistance of more people than I could possibly thank.

My wife, Rola Zaarour, patiently supported me as I disappeared into a cave for several months, encouraging me during moments of borderline despair.

My father, Omar Khalil, served as a tireless one-man research division—constantly suggesting new themes and topics, catching my mistakes, and re-reading the manuscript almost as many times as I did. My brother Hani Khalil provided moral support and a window into the realities of the publishing industry.

My old friend Natasha Ghoneim served as a guardian angel who just might have saved the entire project. When my wife seriously sprained her ankle with a massive deadline looming, Natasha basically moved in with us to help care for her and to buy me some space to write.

ACKNOWLEDGMENTS

Natasha, Rola, and Hani also took turns as my overseas proxy tweeters during the period of the revolution when the Internet was shut down, so many thanks for that as well!

My agent, David Patterson, nurtured the idea from a mere seed to a fully formed proposal and helped smooth over a million little bumps (and defused one or two writer-tantrums) along the way. My editor, Yaniv Soha, patiently coached me through more than one blown deadline, and the entire team at St. Martin's Press handled their duties with professionalism and astonishing speed.

I owe them, and many, many others, my sincere and heartfelt gratitude.

Nathalie Atalla, the marketing executive who is quoted in chapter 17, died in a car accident about two months after we spoke. She left behind two young children. My condolences go out to her family.

AUTHOR'S NOTE

A Note on Transliterations

Moving between Arabic and English spellings is a mystifying process with no set rules. With transliterated names, places, or chants, I have used my own, somewhat instinctive, system designed so that the word will read as phonetically close as possible to its accurate pronunciation.

With formal names, I have tried to keep to a basic template of "al-Name" as in Kasr al-Nil Bridge. Any variations from that template—such as Mohamed ElBaradei or Maha Elgamal—reflect the specific preferences of the people involved as to how they spell their names in English.

PROLOGUE

Cairo Burning

It was January 28, 2011, just before sunset in Cairo, and the tide had dramatically turned against President Hosni Mubarak's police state. Mubarak's once-fearsome band of bullies was being openly hunted in the streets surrounding Tahrir Square, the epicenter of a burgeoning revolution.

A day of increasingly violent street battles had seen tens of thousands of protesters confronting the forces of Central Security—the ground level shock troops of Egypt's monolithic Interior Ministry. A response that started with riot shields, wooden batons, and water cannons had long since escalated into massive tear-gas barrages and the indiscriminate use of buckshot. The protesters, in the face of such violence, temporarily abandoned their signature cries of *salmeya* (peaceful) and responded with their own storm of rocks, concrete chunks, and, eventually, Molotov cocktails.

The combatants in Cairo had no idea what was happening in Alexandria or Suez or any of the hundreds of revolutionary battle zones that day. There was no Internet and no cell phone service—a final desperation move by the government to choke communications and blunt the mounting waves of public anger that threatened to sweep away Mubarak's twenty-nine-year rule. All they knew was what they could see, and what they could see was hundreds of Central Security cadres standing between them and Tahrir.

It was sometime before 6:00 P.M. Tear gas still lingered acridly in the air, and blood spattered the asphalt, which had been gouged and broken up to create fresh projectiles. The protesters on the Kasr al-Nil Bridge, bolstered by waves of newly arrived reinforcements, had succeeded after a four-hour battle in at last cracking police lines.

Everything changed in that moment. In the streets surrounding Tahrir Square, it was now open season on anyone wearing the signature black Central Security uniform.

Ahmad Abdalla, a young film director, crossed the bridge in the immediate aftermath of this victory. He found a scene of bloodlust and revenge. The Central Security cadres that hadn't yet fled had apparently been left to fend for themselves; they were outnumbered, terrified, and viciously targeted by enraged protesters.

"Some people were ready to eat them alive," Abdalla recalled. "There were still a few paddy wagons roaming around. But anytime one would appear, it would immediately get surrounded and pounded with rocks."

Many of the protesters had already been driven half crazy by the violence of the day—and by the twenty-nine years that had preceded it. But mixed in with that rage, there was also a crucial undercurrent of sympathy. Central Security was an easy and natural target, but it wasn't the real target. The underfed and undereducated rural conscripts who made up the regime's frontline cannon fodder generally had had no choice in the matter. As much as any other Egyptian citizen, they were victims of the Mubarak regime. In different circumstances, many of these same soldiers would have been fighting on the side of the protesters. Violently defeating them was a necessary evil, but they were not the real enemy, and even amidst the chaos of the day, many demonstrators on January 28 kept that fact in mind.

As triumphant protesters streamed across the newly liberated Kasr al-Nil Bridge, a Central Security transport truck filled with soldiers emerged from a side street and came flying down the Nile-side Corniche—the broad multilane avenue that lines both side of the Nile. Apparently seeking escape, it didn't stand a chance; protesters immediately surrounded the vehicle in front of the Nile Hilton Hotel—a venerable Cairo landmark that was closed down at the time for a massive renovation. Rocks struck the transport from all sides, causing it to shudder on its axles and lurch forward out of control. The panicked driver crashed hard into the concrete median of an entrance ramp to Kasr al-Nil Bridge.

Jubilant protestors scrambled on board. The driver was injured in the crash and in shock. Bleeding and weeping hysterically, he cried out, "Just kill me. I don't want to live." The back door of the truck was jammed and about a dozen terrified and traumatized Central Security conscripts were trapped inside. There were protesters who clearly wanted to tear the conscripts apart.

But cooler heads prevailed. Abdalla and others extracted the driver and sat him down on a Nile-side bench, literally hugging the semi-coherent man to both console and protect him from other protesters. With the main door jammed, young demonstrators conducted a brief negotiation with the trapped soldiers, speaking through the vehicle's rooftop hatch. Eventually a compromise was reached: the soldiers would be allowed to leave unmolested through the hole in the roof. But there was a condition: they would leave behind their black Central Security uniforms and walk away clad only in their government-issued underwear. The standoff ended amicably (and the Central Security uniforms and equipment made great souvenirs for several dozen protesters).

"They told the soldiers, 'We're not going to let you out unless you take off those clothes,'"Abdalla recalled. "It wasn't exactly a fair negotiation."

It was a small moment that encapsulated the political earthquake transforming the future of the Arab World's most populous and most important country. Similar scenes were playing out all across the nation. In Alexandria, Egypt's second city, the police had already been routed hours earlier and had disappeared from the streets— touching off a festival of joyous destruction, targeting dozens of police stations and all symbols of Mubarak's ruling National Democratic Party.

Egypt was in revolt, and Tahrir Square—the capital's natural and historic heart—had been liberated. The shock troops that had protected Mubarak from his own people had been defeated, forcing the aging autocrat to deal honestly with his citizens for the first time in generations.

Immediately Tahrir (the name means "liberation" in Arabic) became the epicenter of a revolution. Protesters not only transformed it, they were themselves transformed by their presence in it. Tahrir became a revolutionary organism unto itself, bigger than any one citizen or political faction—and most important, bigger than Mubarak and his government.

For the next two weeks, through halfhearted government concessions, media smear campaigns, and violent direct assaults, Egypt's revolutionaries refused to relinquish their hold on Tahrir. As long as they held onto the square, the revolution continued and Mubarak grew weaker. The most dominant chant instantly became: "We won't leave until *he* leaves."

And that's exactly what happened. Mubarak, after twenty-nine years in power, was forced to flee because the Tahrir protesters wouldn't leave and wouldn't accept anything less than the end of his reign.

The Accidental Dictator

Imagine for a moment that President George Bush (the first) had suddenly died in office, leaving Dan Quayle—a national punch line who nobody thought would ever wield any real power—as president of the United States. Then imagine that nearly three decades later, that same perceived lightweight was *still* running the country; that an entire generation of Americans had never known any other leader; that he and Marilyn Quayle were busily renaming public buildings, bridges, and libraries after themselves; and that president-for-life Quayle was seemingly grooming one of his children to continue the family business of running the country.

If that seems far-fetched, it's not too far from the reality that Egyptians had been living through for nearly three decades. Put simply: Hosni Mubarak's era as Egypt's modern-day pharaoh was never supposed to happen. One of the core ironies of Mubarak's twenty-nine-year death grip on Egypt was that he stumbled into what was prob-ably the most important and influential job in the modern Middle East entirely by accident.

It's a reality that became abundantly clear from the very beginning of the eighteen-day uprising in the win-ter of 2011 that finally toppled Mubarak. Once protesters succeeded in shattering the police state that had kept him in power, it became immediately clear that there re-ally was no Plan B. Mubarak's regime, in its final days, fell back on a parade of antiquated, insincere rhetoric, uninspired and tone-deaf concessions, and finally, one last effort at vicious violence in a desperate attempt to retain control.

It all served to underscore that hiding behind the truncheons and tear gas of the Central Security riot po-lice was an intellectually bankrupt and cynical blank space of a regime. That's why there was a distinct under-current of bitterness and shame mixed in with the eu-phoria and the resurgent sense of empowerment coursing through the Cairo streets that February, when Mubarak meekly left the stage.

The sentiment was something approaching: "I can't believe we let *these guys* run our lives for decades."

Mohammed Hosni Mubarak rose to power as much be-cause of what he wasn't as for any particular gifts he possessed. Longtime observers describe him as a sort of Middle Eastern dictatorial Forrest Gump, constantly advancing through a series of happy accidents—being in the right place at the right time.

President Anwar Sadat, who began his reign in 1970, promoted Mubarak from among the ranks of his senior generals due, as much as anything, to his deficiencies. He wasn't regarded as ambitious or particularly intelligent. He wasn't a plotter or a politician. In essence, he wasn't a threat. In an interview early in his reign, Mubarak once quipped that his highest professional ambition had been to one day serve as Egypt's ambassador to the United Kingdom.

"He was just the guy in the back of the photo behind Anwar Sadat that we never thought would be president," said Hisham Kassem, a longtime Egyptian human rights activist and independent publisher. "Basically Sadat wanted somebody to secure the loyalty of the military. He just wanted one of the top generals. Mubarak was the least charismatic and the least interested in politics. So it went to him. Believe me, nobody thought he was going to stick around for thirty years."

Born into a middle-class family (his father was a mid-level Ministry of Justice official) in rural Menoufeya Province on May 4, 1928, young Mubarak had entered the military straight out of high school, and rose through the ranks of the Air Force as a fighter pilot and aviation instructor, eventually becoming commander of the Egyptian Air Force.

His defining moment came in October 1973 when Sadat launched a surprise attack across the Suez Canal and into the Sinai Peninsula, which Israel had occupied since 1967's Six-Day War.

The conflict ended in a military stalemate. By the time a ceasefire was declared, the Israeli forces had recovered from their initial shock and were starting to seize the momentum and advance on Cairo. But psychologically and strategically it was a massive victory for Sadat. The sight of Egyptian troops bravely crossing to the east bank of the canal in the teeth of entrenched Israeli Bar Lev Line helped exorcize the deep emotional traumas of the Six-Day War, when Israel thoroughly trounced multiple Arab armies and permanently stained the legacy of Sadat's predecessor, the iconic Gamal Abdel Nasser. Strategically, the conflict frightened Israel enough that Sadat was later able to negotiate with the Jewish state from a position of strength.

Mubarak came out of the 1973 conflict a war hero, although there were, in later years, allegations that his actual strategic role in the conflict was retroactively exaggerated. "There were ten or twelve other [military commanders] who played a larger role," said Hassan Nafaa, a Cairo University political science professor who emerged in Mubarak's final years in power as a prominent regime critic. Whatever the truth, Sadat packaged his air force commander as one of the faces of victory and promoted him to vice president in 1975.

Sadat and his protégé were a study in contrasts. Sadat was wily, bold, vain, and mercurial—prone to emotional instability and temper tantrums, but also undeniably clever. Mubarak was none of the above.

For several years, Mubarak lurked in the shadows behind the charismatic Sadat, a vaguely recognizable face standing behind the president as he delivered a speech or met with foreign dignitaries. He was handsome in a stocky, square-jawed sort of way, looked good in a suit, and seemed to be one of the few who were privy to Sadat's inner counsels. But beyond that he didn't make much of an impression on either the local or international stage. There's a common story (possibly apocryphal) that when Henry Kissinger first met Mubarak with Sadat, he thought Mubarak was some sort of junior aid, not the country's vice president. Even within local military circles and in the public eye, he was dwarfed by more charismatic figures such as powerful defense minister Abdel Halim Abu Ghazala.

On October 6, 1981, Sadat was killed by an Islamist cell inside his own army, ironically during a parade to commemorate his 1973 military victory. The preceding years had seen Sadat demonstrate his trademark tendency for both bold unilateral moves and thin-skinned impetuousness. In the wake of the 1973 war, Sadat stunned the nation and the region by suddenly launching open peace negotiations with Israel. His landmark decision to visit Jerusalem on November 20, 1977, led to the Camp David Peace Accords with Israel and to Egypt's near-total isolation from the rest of the Arab World.

Sadat's gambit placed Egypt firmly in the American camp during the height of the Cold War, ensuring an annual flow of billions in U.S. aid that continue to this day. But it also inflamed local hostility toward Israel and made Egypt a regional pariah. In 1979, the Arab League expelled Egypt and moved its headquarters from Cairo to Tunis. While Sadat was hailed internationally as a bold statesman, he was regarded in the Arab world as having repudiated Nasser's vision of Arab nationalism and cut a deal to place Egypt's interests above those of the wider Arab community.

Domestically, he became increasingly oppressive and erratic in response to his critics; in September 1981, he launched a massive internal crackdown, rounding up and imprisoning more than fifteen hundred perceived dissidents. The victims included not just militant Islamists—regarded as the primary threat—but intellectuals and activists of all ideological stripes. Even the Coptic Christian Pope Shenouda III was placed under house arrest in a monastery, and dozens of priests were arrested.

But Sadat's crackdown missed a jihadi cell within his own army led by Lt. Khaled Islambouli. When the assassins struck, Mubarak was standing right next to Sadat. Despite the presidential reviewing stand being peppered by bullets and grenades, Mubarak miraculously managed to escape with just a minor hand injury. It's an enduring testament to Mubarak's lack of regard by the nation that there was never any serious speculation that he had been in on the plot. Despite being the most obvious beneficiary of Sadat's assassination, many Egyptians simply refused to believe he was clever or ambitious enough to pull off—or even conceive of—a coup.

In the wake of Sadat's assassination, there was no guarantee that Mubarak would automatically ascend to the presidency. A handful of senior military leaders could have laid claim to the throne, particularly the aforementioned Defense Minister Abu Ghazala, but also senior general Saad Mamoun and Kamal Hassan Ali, the Foreign Minister and former head of intelligence.

Kassem, the independent publisher, calls it yet another happy accident that smoothed Mubarak's path into the presidential palace. If Sadat had died of a heart attack or in a plane crash, he posits, the Mubarak era never would have started in the first place.

"Abu Ghazala had a towering presence. He was much more popular and publicly known than Mubarak," Kassem said. "I think he would have succeeded Sadat if only Sadat hadn't been killed in a military parade. That's what made Abu Ghazala's ascension politically impossible. The conspiracy theory would have prevailed that Abu Ghazala killed Sadat."

Instead, a slightly stunned nation suddenly found itself under the leadership of a lightly regarded nonentity. But despite being widely perceived as not really up to the job, Mubarak entered the presidency on a moderate wave of public goodwill. Once again, he benefited from what he was not. Sadat groomed and elevated Mubarak because he wasn't as charismatic and ambitious as some of the military peers; Egyptians cautiously embraced him, at first, purely because he wasn't Sadat.

Life under Anwar Sadat was an exhausting roller-coaster ride for many. He launched bold initiatives, switched camps between the United States and Soviet Union on a whim, responded harshly to almost any sort of criticism, restructured the economy away from Nasser's socialist model, and dragged the country into sometimes unpopular directions. Mubarak was stolid, cautious, and a little unimaginative—qualities that made him a much-needed calming influence in those early years. He seemed disciplined, hardworking, and sincere—the Good Cop to Sadat's unstable and irrational Bad Cop.

"Mostly, the people were just happy that Sadat was gone. Either way, the general feeling was that [Mubarak] wouldn't last long," said Nafaa.

"He was all right at the beginning. People felt he was cautious and trying to move the country forward," said Mohammed ElBaradei, the former head of the International Atomic Energy Agency, who later emerged as one of Mubarak's most high-profile critics. At the time of Mubarak's ascension, ElBaradei had just left the Egyptian Foreign Ministry and was in New York beginning what would become a thirty-year career with the United Nations. Decades later, he would meet Mubarak several times as head of the IAEA. ElBaradei said he found President Mubarak "extremely friendly and informal" but felt that "[h]e had no sense of a grand vision or imagination."

In typical Egyptian fashion the Mubarak jokes started immediately. Dark humor is one of the defining Egyptian characteristics and nobody is spared. My father, who immigrated to the United States in 1968, often told me that Nasser would deploy intelligence officers in coffee shops across the country just to monitor the jokes being swapped over tea and shisha pipes. Nasser-era jokes typically centered on the brutal way his internal security forces dealt with dissidents. Sadat was subjected to an endless stream of jokes about his long-rumored passion for hashish and about how Kissinger had repeatedly outsmarted him during the Nixon years.

In Mubarak's case, most of the jokes revolved around his perceived lack of intelligence. He was instantly dubbed *La Vache Qui Rit* or "The Laughing Cow," after a popular brand of French packaged cheese available in every market.

Here's an example of an early-period Mubarak joke:

> *The new president conducts an official visit to a prototype Ministry of Agriculture cattle ranch that breeds livestock from around the world.*
>
> *The director takes him around and shows him the first animal, "This is a Friesian from Holland, Mr. President," then the second, "This is an angus steer from America," then the third, "This is a water buffalo from India," and so on . . . Somewhere along the tour, Mubarak stops and points asking, "And what is this one?" The guide answers sheepishly, "This is a mirror, Mr. President."*

Despite such inauspicious beginnings, Mubarak actually seemed to start off his reign on the right foot. He immediately released most of the detainees jailed in Sadat's final tantrum-fueled crackdowns. He pledged not to stay more than two presidential terms. He hosted a high-profile conference of prominent economists in an effort to design a new economic vision for the country going forward. And he, memorably, launched an anticorruption campaign, jailing several prominent regime-connected businessmen—including Alexandria tycoon Rashad Osman and Sadat's own brother Esmat. In retrospect, that seems likely to have been a more cynical ploy to clear out Sadat's power brokers, and to make way for his own cadre. But at the time, many Egyptians wanted to believe he was sincere.

"Of course like any new leader, there was wishful thinking," said Wael Khalil, a longtime socialist activist and blogger who was one of the quiet architects of Egypt's revolution. Khalil (no relation to the author) was in high school when Mubarak assumed the presidency. "You didn't have any say anyway, so you can only hope that he's honest."

In a defining moment of his early years (one that drips with irony in retrospect), Mubarak made a public speech announcing, "The death shroud doesn't have pockets." Translation: You can't take it with you.

Domestically, Mubarak faced immediate problems, with the ongoing threat of militant Islamist groups and with his country's crumbling infrastructure. The Islamists were dealt with through a combination of an ongoing (and generally popular) security crackdown that drove them out of the capital and into the rural south, and by continuing Sadat's policy of quietly encouraging radical youth to seek their jihadist dreams in Afghanistan. The infrastructure issues were partially handled through the now-blossoming post–Camp David relationship with the United States. In one case, a survey of the

Cairo sewer system revealed that the capital was just a few years away from being knee-deep in sewage. A multi-million-dollar U.S. initiative completely remade the Cairo sewage network, allowing Mubarak to demonstrate to his people the immediate "peace dividend" of the Camp David accords.

Much of Mubarak's foreign policy centered on cementing the ties Sadat had built with Washington. This was the beginning of what would be a decades-long relationship that saw Egypt's security forces and military become deeply intertwined with their U.S. counterparts. American military hardware and aid began flowing into Cairo and generations of police and army officers began receiving advanced training in the United States. The largesse would continue as long as Mubarak kept to the terms of Camp David and controlled his people's dissatisfaction over the plight of the Palestinians.

"He really threw himself in the lap of the Americans, far more than Sadat," said Kassem. "He knew that the best guarantee for the regime was that the Americans were satisfied, and he really strengthened his relations with the CIA and the Pentagon. These were his strategic relations—not the Congress or the White House because these things come and go."

The deepening dependence on Washington—and the significant parallel costs to Egypt's regional prestige in the Arab world, stirred up limited (and easily controlled) domestic opposition. Most of the criticism at this point was about Mubarak's dependency on (and perceived subservience to) the United States and its interests.

By the end of the 1980s, Mubarak had largely succeeded in entrenching his position. Abu Ghazala, his most powerful potential rival, was ousted from the defense ministry in 1989, ending the possibility of serious challenges from within the regime. Externally, 1989 also marked the year when the Arab League finally "forgave" Egypt for its Camp David betrayal, re-admitting the country to its ranks, and relocated its headquarters back to its traditional home in Cairo.

Mubarak's second defining moment as president came ten years into his reign when a dispute over shared oil fields led Iraqi dictator Saddam Hussein to invade and occupy the tiny Arabian Gulf monarchy of Kuwait. From the very start of the dispute, Egypt was an enthusiastic partner in U.S. President George Bush's campaign to oust Hussein from Kuwait. Mubarak's support helped provide regional legitimacy and bring other Arab nations on board, and forty-five-thousand Egyptian troops played an active role in the ensuing Gulf War.

Mubarak's vocal support for the U.S. campaign only deepened the local perception of him among opposition circles as an American puppet. But there were probably deeper and more complicated reasons at work as well. Cairo and Baghdad have jostled for centuries over cultural and political dominance of the Arab world—a historic rivalry that may have played into Mubarak's eagerness to see the ascendant and aggressive Hussein weakened.

There was also a significant financial incentive at

play. Egypt had been struggling under crippling debt to the IMF and major western powers; during the late 1980s the country was at serious risk of defaulting on billions of dollars in loans. In 1990–1991, Egypt's fiscal deficit was running at 20 percent of GDP, inflation was soaring, and foreign-debt service was consuming fifty cents of every dollar received. That grim economic picture changed immediately after the first Persian Gulf War. As a reward for Mubarak's participation in the anti-Saddam coalition, America, the Gulf States, and Europe collectively forgave Egypt about $20 billion-worth of debt and rescheduled a nearly equal amount. The end result was a new financial lease on life for Mubarak's government, and a suddenly rosy economic picture.

These were the Golden Years for Mubarak. His National Democratic Party (NDP) had a firm grip on the executive and legislative branches of government. The judicial branch remained a bit of an enduring thorn in the government's side, with Egypt's judges proving remarkably resistant to co-option; but it rarely amounted to more than an annoyance. A small handful of toothless opposition parties were permitted, mainly to provide democratic window dressing. They could even produce their own opposition newspapers, where they could criticize government corruption and embarrass ministers—as long as they never mentioned the name "Mubarak" in anything less than respectful terms. The so-called Emergency Laws, imposed by Sadat, that granted sweeping powers of arrest and detention—and which would come to play a significant role in Mubarak's ouster in 2011—were repeatedly renewed by the rubber-stamp parliament.

Mubarak was re-elected via heavily stage-managed national referendums in 1987 and 1993. Suddenly, against all odds, the Laughing Cow was in the clear and fully in control.

2

Signposts on the Way to Tahrir

How exactly do you pinpoint the moment when an already unjust and undemocratic regime starts to go really bad? When does the toxic rot start to truly settle in? A dozen Egyptians could probably give you that many responses. Hosni Mubarak's Egypt was never a just or democratic place. But there are degrees of oppression and injustice. And somewhere along the line Mubarak's government crossed over to a truly dark place.

Let's be clear here: Hosni Mubarak was never as brutal, ruthless, or sadistic as some of his contemporaries, like Saddam Hussein or Hafez El Assad. As modern dictators go, he would struggle even to make the Top 10. There will be no Iraq-style revelations of mass graves in Egypt. Instead, Mubarak's ultimate crime will be treating his people with contempt—openly disrespecting them for so long that many Egyptians lost both respect for

themselves and the sense that they could change anything that was happening around them.

Mubarak's reign had a genuinely corrosive effect on
Egypt's society and psyche. He took a proud and ancient
civilization and presided over the virtual collapse of its
citizens' sense of public empowerment and political engagement. He taught them how to feel helpless, then made
them forget they had ever felt any other way. His reign
spread cynicism, apathy, and, eventually, self-loathing.

Several successive generations were instilled with the
belief that the system was rotten to the core, and that
there was nothing anyone could do about it. Anyone who
tried to change that dynamic was regarded as a noble
fool. Egyptians were taught to "walk next to the wall"—
translation: Keep your head down, feed your family, and
don't stick your nose in affairs of governance that are
above your station.

The larger tale of Mubarak's Egypt is that of a government that worked hard (and rather successfully) to convince the majority of its people that resistance was futile
and that there was no point in trying to change or im-
prove their circumstances. Having largely accomplished
that task, it then proceeded to place this demoralized
population in such desperate and intolerable circumstances that it re-politicized them all over again.

One indisputably significant moment, and perhaps a line
of demarcation, was on November 17, 1997, the day of the
Luxor Massacre.

That morning, Islamist gunmen invaded the poorly guarded temple of Queen Hatshepsut in southern Egypt. Dressed as security officers, they easily overwhelmed the temple guards and began methodically killing tourists. Despite Egypt's status as a highly developed and effective police state, the response from local security forces was tragically slow. According to eyewitness accounts, the gunmen were able to spend the next forty-five minutes casually hunting down and murdering tourists in the massive temple complex with machine guns and machetes before the first police officers arrived on the scene. All told, fifty-eight foreign tourists died, along with three Egyptian police officers and one tour guide.

To the observer, it was like an earthquake had struck; people were absolutely horrified. Many felt personally ashamed. Courtesy and hospitality to guests is sort of an oft-repeated Arab world cliché, but it's also largely true; Luxor represented not only savage cruelty to Egypt's visitors but also seemed maliciously designed to ensure that the vital flow of cash-spending foreign tourists would dry up indefinitely. For months afterward, the empty stores of the once-bustling Khan al-Khalili bazaar displayed heartbreaking handmade signs in the windows literally begging in multiple languages for the world's tourists to return.

The Luxor Massacre had two immediate effects. First it crippled whatever lingering popular sentiment existed in society toward the various armed Islamic militant groups—much like the Oklahoma City bombing helped destroy sympathy for America's domestic militia movement.

The other key result of Luxor was that it launched the reign of Interior Minister Habib al-Adly.

In the wake of the massacre, Mubarak rushed to the scene and wasted no time holding his underlings accountable. In a moment of grand theater, he essentially fired his Interior Minister Hassan al-Alfy live on television in front of the accompanying international press corps. In his place came al-Adly, a small, tidy man who had the aspect more of an accountant than an all-powerful security chief. Al-Adly had previously headed up the Mubaheth Amn al-Dawla, or State Security Investigations Bureau—the ministry's highest investigative authority with a mandate to protect against threats to national security. The new minister was given a brief to secure the country from the armed Islamist threat, no questions asked.

Throughout the late 1990s and turn of the century, his cadres brutally confronted militant Islamist groups. The campaign was largely met with public approval, but in the process something darker happened. Egypt's police became an unchecked and unchallenged law unto themselves, with State Security mushrooming in power and extending its influence into almost every aspect of Egyptian life. Opposition politicians, newspaper editors, university professors, judges, and prominent businessmen— all of them eventually fell under the gaze of State Security.

"Amn al-Dawla was dictating and controlling things— who could speak at public meetings, the media, the universities. They really were running the country," said Wael Khalil, who came of age as a socialist political organizer during the Mubarak years. "It really deteriorated in the last ten years. You didn't need to be an activist or have a quarrel with the state to be targeted. You could 'walk next to the wall' and still be beaten to death."

Even within the police force itself, State Security's rapidly expanding grasp on society was a source of controversy and resentment. Gen. Ahmed Khalil, a former head of criminal investigations for the rural West Nile Delta province of Beheira, described State Security as "an octopus" which came to dominate the Ministry of Interior and eventually the entire government.

"They were everywhere and into everything," said Khalil (full disclosure: he's a distant relative of the author). "They controlled labor syndicate elections, they approved or rejected newspaper editors, they decided who could serve as head of a university department, they even got involved in elections for student government. . . . That's when the police state really started."[1]

Gen. Khalil was eager to blame the regime's abuses on State Security, while portraying the mainstream police force as innocent victims of the same oppressive system. Egypt's police, he claimed, were overworked, disrespected, and misused during the final decade of Mubarak's reign— unwillingly cast in the role of literal Bad Cops.

---

1 Gen. Khalil's sentiments can be taken with a grain of salt; during a pair of long, sometimes confrontational, interviews, he frequently expressed bitterness about how State Security's ascendance brought with it a parallel loss of prestige for mainstream police officers such as himself within the ministry. "A first lieutenant in State Security would march in and order around a police general," he complained. "There was nothing we could do."

"It was always security solutions to political problems, so the police became oppressors," he said. "The work of the police began to be split between protecting the citizens and protecting the regime. The last ten years [under Mubarak] was 100 percent about protecting the regime. . . . This revolution was always coming. It was probably ten years too late."

With no real checks on their behavior, the internal culture of Egypt's security forces deteriorated rapidly. Supported on paper by the Emergency Laws, and backed by the full power of all aspects of the government, the police devolved into Egypt's largest and most heavily armed criminal mob. The entire relationship of the police to society changed and warped.

"All Egyptians had to enter a police station at some point," said Haitham Mesbah, a supervisor at a clothing factory in Alexandria and a close friend of Khaled Saieed—the young man whose public beating death at the hands of police in June 2010 helped galvanize citizens and laid one of the final seeds for the revolution. "There's not a single Egyptian who entered a police station without some sort of garbage happening. At the very least [you] would have to pay a bribe. You would be walking down the street and they take your ID card and it costs you LE20 to get it back. At some point, it just became a gang."

Exactly how much Mubarak knew or cared about the day-to-day behavior of his Ministry of Interior remains an open question. In late 2010, just a few months before the revolution, the Wikileaks organization released a batch of diplomatic cables between the U.S. State Department and its embassies abroad. In one particularly revealing communiqué, former Ambassador to Cairo Margaret Scobey gave her impression that Mubarak trusted al-Adly to maintain order and control and didn't ask too many questions as long as he delivered results.

Scobey's May 2009 cable concluded that Mubarak relied entirely on al-Adly and long-serving intelligence chief Omar Suleiman to "keep the domestic beasts at bay, and Mubarak is not one to lose sleep over their tactics."

With no sincere oversight over Interior Ministry abuses, the situation on the ground became toxic. The police in Mubarak's final decade degenerated into a predatory force, sowing seeds of resentment that would dramatically blossom during the revolution. Ordinary citizens stopped expecting them to perform even the most basic functions of public service or ordinary community protection. They were something to be avoided, never depended upon. If you were in trouble in Egypt, the last place you would look for help was the police.

"In some cases, a teacher would go to report his car being stolen, and the officer at the police station would be in a bad mood. The next thing you know the teacher is arrested and being tortured," said Kassem, who reviewed dozens of such cases during a several-year stint as head of the Egyptian Organization for Human Rights. "This was of course combined with a complete blind government backing for anything the police did."

Mubarak, meanwhile, had gone from the guy nobody thought would be around for long to the guest at the party who refuses to leave. He was omnipresent—and seemingly healthy as a horse, famously playing squash several times a week well into his sixties. Even the jokes changed. The first Mubarak joke I learned upon moving to Egypt in 1997 reflects that changing perception—mixing in the old tropes about his IQ with the growing frustration about his longevity and seeming determination to outlive us all.

It went something like this:

> Shortly after Scottish scientists announced they had successfully cloned a sheep named Dolly, Mubarak read the news and decided this was the perfect solution. He would make clones of himself and that way ensure that Hosni Mubarak leads Egypt forever.
>
> He called in the best scientists in Egypt; they took a sample from his skin cells and ran it through their cloning machinery . . . and out came a donkey. Mubarak went ballistic and screamed at his scientists. Finally he decided to go to Scotland to enlist the help of the original scientists who cloned Dolly.
>
> It was a success! Out of the machine came a perfect walking, talking clone of Hosni Mubarak.
>
> Mubarak was amazed and asked the scientists how they succeeded when the others had failed. They replied, "It was easy, Mr. President. We just used a skin cell sample from a donkey."

3

"And What If We Say 'No'?"

Mubarak entered the twenty-first century seemingly in full command of his nation. In September 1999, Egyptians witnessed the unforgettable spectacle of the nation's final single-candidate presidential referendum. As with the previous votes in 1987 and 1993, the outcome was never in doubt; it wasn't even really the point of the exercise. The point was to burnish Mubarak's legacy as he completed his second decade in power—glorifying him in a manner that would have done his pharaonic predecessors proud.

This time the regime really pulled out all the stops. The months that preceded the vote featured an orgy of praise for the president so completely over the top that it would have made Saddam Hussein blush with embarrassment. As always, the NDP-controlled parliament was tasked with the job of choosing a candidate who would be presented to the country in a national yes/no referendum.

Ruling party MPs competed for who could be more florid in their praise of Mubarak, with some hysterically threatening on the floor of the People's Assembly to cut themselves and sign a loyalty oath to Mubarak in their own blood. He was re-nominated by a vote of 445-0, with only the nine representatives of a tame leftist opposition party abstaining. Nobody had the nerve to vote No.

In the weeks before the "vote," the state-owned flagship *Al-Ahram* newspaper was filled every day with dozens of full-page ads taken out by politicians, professional syndicates, and prominent businessmen—all of them lyrically praising Mubarak as "The Hero of War and Peace" and the "Father of the Nation." At a party-organized pro-Mubarak rally one night, several hundred bussed-in civil servants chanted, "Oh Mubarak who is he?/He is the beloved of the Egyptians." They distributed a poster depicting Mubarak's face on cheap fake papyrus—casting him as a literal pharaoh without the smallest shred of irony.

One day, about two weeks before the vote, I stood on a street in Mohandessin waiting for a microbus—a sort of mass transit minivan that runs set routes and seats about fourteen people—to take me home. A massive, newly installed video screen towered over a nearby busy intersection playing an endless loop of President Hosni Mubarak's greatest hits: Mubarak surveying reclaimed desert farmland, inaugurating Cairo's landmark subway system, and presiding over the turnover of the final piece of Israeli-captured Sinai Peninsula land. At the end, the message flashed: "Yes to Mubarak!"

A man waiting next to me rolled his eyes and muttered, "And what if we said 'No'? Who would we even say no to?" Then a moment later he added, "But between you and me, he's been good. He's done a lot of things."

That sort of cynical ambivalence seemed to characterize the nation under Mubarak during that era. Even his supporters couldn't help but crack jokes about how they didn't really have a choice in the matter. He was never revered the way Nasser was; at best he was accepted as a decent enough guy who seemed to be trying his best. Mostly people couldn't think of a better option, and the government worked hard to make sure than no plausible better options emerged. Multiple observers told me that year that if the 1999 referendum had been a real and fair multicandidate contest, Mubarak probably would have taken 60 percent of the vote—a solid mandate by Western democratic standards.

Shortly before the vote, I sat down with Muhammed al-Sayed Saieed, a political analyst with the government-run Al-Ahram Center for Political and Strategic Studies. I had thought that being a government employee, Saieed would offer a spirited defense of Mubarak to bring balance to the opposition criticism filling my notebooks. Instead Saieed, who passed away in 2009, described Mubarak as basically ruling via apathy.

"People do tend to like him. He's liked, but with no enthusiasm," Saieed told me, adding that he expected voter turnout to be practically nonexistent. "He's not deeply hated, nor profoundly loved."

That was, in retrospect, probably the high-water mark for Mubarak's grip on authority in Egypt. Starting from 2000, things started to go steadily south, as a string of events and decisions began to eat away at Mubarak's domestic power base, regional prestige and even the once rock-solid relations with his primary patrons in Washington, D.C.

On June 30, 2000, more than thirty State Security officers surrounded the home of Saad Eddin Ibrahim, a sociology professor at the American University in Cairo. The sixty-one-year-old academic was held without formal charges for weeks, then eventually prosecuted for a nebulous array of crimes including financial improprieties, forgery, accepting foreign funding without government permission, and seeking to ruin Egypt's international reputation. "All that was left out was drug dealing and rape," Ibrahim joked in an interview shortly after his first release from custody.

The government's smoking gun was a seemingly innocuous European Union–funded short film that Ibrahim's Ibn Khaldoun Center for Developmental Studies was producing to encourage voter participation in parliamentary elections scheduled for that fall. He had also ruffled high-level feathers by speaking publicly about polling place violations in previous elections.

Ibrahim spent years fending off the charges. In a slightly farcical dynamic, the government repeatedly proved that it didn't have enough evidence to get Ibrahim convicted in a normal court, so it kept referring him to specially created State Security Courts, where the state had more control over the process and the selection of compliant judges. But eventually Ibrahim's case would have to enter the mainstream legal system on appeal, where the judges would essentially laugh it out of the room. Twice he was sentenced to long prison terms by State Security Courts, and twice the case died on appeal. Finally a third trial reached the Court of Cassation, the country's highest civil court, which cleared Ibrahim of all charges in 2003.

The case was accompanied by a vicious media smear campaign depicting local NGOs like the Ibn Khaldoun Center as tools for sinister foreign interests, playing into the long-standing public passion for spotting conspiracies around every corner. Moustafa Bakri, then editor in chief of *Al-Osboa* (*The Week*) newspaper and one of the main government attack dogs during this era, was one of the most influential leaders of this anti-NGO campaign. In an editorial, Bakri labeled Ibrahim and his peers "The Trojan Horses of the West," who were seeking to sow dissension, weaken the government, and undermine Egyptian society.

The legal ordeal and multiple stints in jail took their toll on his health and Ibrahim really wasn't the same after that—spending much of the ensuing decade in self-imposed exile, teaching in the United States.

What made the case so puzzling was that Ibrahim was hardly a fire-breathing regime critic. In fact he was regarded by many within the activist and civil society communities as uncomfortably close to the government. But his Ibn Khaldoun Center was one of a handful of local NGOs conducting training for election monitors for parliamentary elections coming up that fall. The lingering impression in the NGO community was that Ibrahim's arrest was designed as a warning shot across their bow—a message for them to mind their own business and make them afraid to accept any foreign funding lest they receive the same treatment. By prosecuting Ibrahim—a dual U.S./Egyptian citizen and a fixture on the international lecture circuit—the government was targeting the biggest fish in the pond to send a message that nobody was safe.

"Somebody thought about this for a while, and chose the right time," Hafez Abu Saada, secretary general of the Egyptian Organization for Human Rights, the country's largest and oldest civil rights group, told me that summer. "It's a complete plan to attack civil society in Egypt."

The Ibrahim case demonstrated both the regime's sensitivity about the growing number of independent local NGOs and civil society groups emerging on the scene, and also its absolute confidence that it could arrest a dual U.S./Egyptian citizen here without lasting harm to its relationship with Washington. The State Department and the local embassy made all the right noises about rule of law and due process. But in the end, the regime gambled correctly that its strategic regional importance and tight relations with the Pentagon would allow it to openly intimidate its own democracy advocates with little consequence.

"I know my case had a dampening effect on civil society," Ibrahim told me in a post-jail interview. "I'm an eternal optimist and I've been looking for signs to fuel my optimism and so far I haven't seen any."

It was a sobering lesson for the country's already beleaguered civic organizations. Abu Saada called the Ibrahim case a demoralizing blow that left NGOs and human rights groups hesitant to accept even the most harmless form of foreign aid for fear of leaving themselves vulnerable to similar treatment. At the time of our interview in 2000, his EOHR was already facing financial problems and staff salaries were being delayed—meanwhile a $25,000 grant offer was on the table from the Dutch development agency NOVIB that his board was now reluctant to accept.

EOHR Board Member Negad al-Borai sounded a similarly bleak note. "I can't see any future for real Egyptian civil society if this continues," he said. "We'll see some [opposition] parties and labor unions here and there, but nothing that can be called true civil society."

But despite his disillusionment, al-Borai and his fellow activists sounded more than willing to continue their fight, even if it meant eventually succumbing to the same treatment that Ibrahim received. That dedication to a noble but thankless cause in the face of overwhelming odds deserves to be lauded in Egypt's revolutionary history books. Long before there was a Kefaya or an April 6 movement or a Khaled Saieed Facebook page, the parties credited with inciting revolution, there were organizations like the EOHR and the Hisham Mubarak Law Center and the Nedim Center for the Rehabilitation of

Violence and Torture Victims, who fought the good fight and who suffered mightily in comparative obscurity for decades.

"We will continue our struggle against this corrupt government. We will continue to speak for democracy—with foreign funding or without, from inside or outside the prison," al-Borai told me back in 2000. "We will accept the results. I am ready for prison. At least it will give me some rest."

Throughout the late '90s and early part of the twenty-first century, activists managed to stage a series of public protests—but they were almost always focused on foreign policy issues such as Israel, and they were always easily dispatched by Central Security—the baton-wielding shock troops of the Interior Ministry. The start of the Second Palestinian Intifada in September 2000 kicked off one of these hot periods of bubbling protest action. Ordinary citizens were enraged by scenes of the Israeli Army confronting outgunned and overmatched stone-throwing Palestinian youth—and further disgruntled by the presence of an Israeli embassy in the heart of Cairo.

But this period of domestic unrest also served to underscore several disturbing realities for the activists and protesters: The activists themselves were not on the same page. The security forces had the unrest completely under their control. And ordinary apolitical citizens, no matter how much they agreed, were too busy or too scared to join in.

Among the protesters, much of the internal conflict centered around whether or not to turn their frustrations with Israel against the Mubarak regime. This was the tail end of the period when the Mubarak name was still basically sacred, and any direct criticism of the president or his family, either verbally or in print, was an invitation to a jail cell.

"I remember in 2001 at a protest when some of us wanted to chant 'Hosni Mubarak, you collaborator' and others would tell us 'No, that's too much,'" said Wael Khalil, the longtime socialist activist.

I attended several such protests during this period, mostly based on the grounds of Cairo University, and witnessed this phenomenon firsthand. In general terms, the socialists and liberal protesters favored direct criticism of the regime and calling Mubarak out by name; the Islamist protesters argued that this was too dangerous and that it was better to keep things focused on Israel.

Either way, the protests never amounted to more than a noisy distraction, and the Central Security forces grew extremely proficient at keeping things bottled up. Occasionally, they would have to resort to tear gas, usually when the Cairo University students attempted to march off the walled confines of their campus. But even the occasional street battle never truly threatened the dominion of the police state. The Cairo University campus is less than three blocks away from the Israeli embassy;

with a pair of binoculars, you can literally see the Israeli flag flapping in the breeze while standing on the university grounds. For months, every Intifada-related protest at the university would eventually evolve into an attempted march on the embassy. Despite dozens of attempts, the students never got close.

The final harsh reality of this period of activism, and what most significantly differentiated it from the protests of 2011, was that the larger Egyptian population—despite sympathizing deeply with the Palestinians—were not willing to defy their government by joining in.

I vividly recall covering a day of scattered protests back in 2002. Demonstrators, mainly young students, were enraged over the latest Israeli crackdown. My long-time home in Cairo's Giza district is walking distance from both Cairo University and the Israeli embassy, which often gave me a front-row seat to countless protest marches.

On the day in question, I stood on the sidewalk watching a phalanx of black-clad Central Security officers scatter a group of young protesters and chase them down Mourad Street, a block from my apartment. I asked a local shopkeeper what he thought of the scene and his response haunted me: "If we had any dignity, we would be with them."

That rather depressing scenario repeated itself again and again, developing its own familiar rhythm. Protests of two or three hundred people—many of them familiar faces from the last six protests—would gather at the university, or at the Lawyers Syndicate or Journalists

Syndicate downtown. Central Security would deploy in overwhelming numbers, often at a 5-1 advantage over the protesters. There would be chanting, maybe some pushing and shoving along the front lines. Occasionally the riot police would calculatedly let a particularly aggressive group of youth push through their lines—then close ranks behind them and beat them mercilessly. Eventually the older hands in the activist ranks would start negotiations with their counterparts among the security officers and everyone would be allowed to go home. In the aftermath of a particularly disruptive protest, some of the usual suspect ringleaders would be rounded up and detained for questioning, touching off another round of protests in their defense. The protesters, security officers, and journalists all knew each other. It started to feel like some sort of Kabuki theater—an elaborate dance with everyone playing their prescribed role, as the Cairo traffic rolled obliviously past.

Then on March 20, 2003, something amazing happened, shaking up that grindingly familiar dynamic. On the night that the U.S.-led coalition launched its invasion of Iraq, enraged protesters in Cairo actually overwhelmed the security forces for the first time in the Mubarak era and took over Tahrir Square for a night. Mubarak had publicly opposed the buildup to the invasion, warning that it would have disastrous results. But many Egyptians saw that as mere public posturing, designed to save face. When Mubarak permitted American warships to sail through the Suez Canal to take up positions for the invasion, popular sentiment viewed him as a tool of imperialism.

I was in Qatar at the time covering CentCom, the American military's command center, and watched on television scenes I never thought would be possible in Egypt—Central Security overmatched, outnumbered, and on the run; jubilant protesters carrying riot batons and Plexiglas shields as souvenirs.

This first occupation of Tahrir is something of a forgotten footnote in modern Egyptian history, but for those who were involved, it was a key turning point on the road to revolution.

"That was more or less an embryo, a rehearsal for January 28," said Wael Khalil, who participated in the protests. There was no lasting occupation that time; protesters basically held a boisterous several-hour rally and dispersed after midnight. But the experience provided a massive confidence boost for Egypt's beleaguered activist forces. It was one of the first times that popular anger over foreign policy issues had publicly turned inward against the regime.

"The tone of anti-Mubarak sentiment and the focus on the question of democracy really started then," Khalil said. "It started with 'Down with America' and turned to 'Down with Mubarak.'"

More than eight years later, Khalil still grins when he recalls seeing the crowds that night tear down a massive poster of Mubarak hanging outside the NDP headquarters on the edge of Tahrir Square.

"I was excited like a child," he said. "To me, Mubarak never regained legitimacy after that."

That was the first time in decades that the Mubarak regime looked as though it was faltering. The March 20 protests were immediately followed by a sweeping crackdown and roundup of many of the activists involved, but Mubarak's emboldened domestic opponents seemed determined to press their advantage.

One quick anecdote from my own professional experience to illustrate this crucial shift in Mubarak's prestige: In autumn 2002, I had finished a one-year stint as editor in chief of the seminal weekly English-language newsmagazine *Cairo Times* and stepped down to became a contributing writer. Hisham Kassem was my publisher and my successor as editor was Issandr El Amrani—now a prominent regional analyst and founder of the influential Arabist blog. At the time, Gamal Mubarak, the president's investment banker son, was making one of his first steps toward true power, framed around the upcoming annual National Democratic Party conference. Gamal was positioned as the young internal reformer battling the NDP "old guard" for the soul and future of the party. Newspapers, including the state-owned media, hyped the internal struggle in terms reminiscent of a pro-wrestling steel-cage grudge match.

I wrote an article for *Cairo Times* about the preconference hype and its implications for Gamal's much-rumored presidential aspirations. At the last minute, on production night, Kassem told me to strip out all mention of the Gamal succession scenario—which, I argued, killed the relevance of the article. I eventually walked out in a huff, leaving poor Issandr to gut my article.

In recalling that fight years later, Kassem told me he was simply reading the shifting political winds and deciding on instinct what he could get away with. He sensed that pushing the "President Gamal" possibilities at this delicate stage would get the *Cairo Times* banned or otherwise punished. Kassem recalled that within a few months, he shifted strategy, after sensing the regime's growing vulnerability. Like Wael Khalil, he points to the March 2003 Iraq invasion as a turning point.

In the final lead-up to the war, a handful of Egyptian intellectuals and activists published an open letter, harshly and personally criticizing Mubarak and his handling of the situation. By now, Paul Schemm—now a Morocco-based correspondent for the Associated Press—was the *Cairo Times* editor, and Kassem asked Paul to commission a story about the new opposition to Mubarak.

Schemm asked, "Are you going to make us work on it and then kill it on production night? You've never allowed us to touch Mubarak."

"I told him, 'I know what I'm doing,'" Kassem recalled. "And we did the story and got away with it . . . It was clear [Mubarak] was in a weakened position. By the end of that year things had gotten out of control completely for him. People were personally attacking him left and right."

Later that same year, Egyptians faced the equally unprecedented vision of Mubarak himself looking physically weak. On November 19, 2003, the seventy-five-year-old president collapsed while giving a televised speech in Parliament. He received medical attention for about forty-five minutes, then returned to the parliament floor, to a rapturous reception, to finish his speech. The official story released by the media was that Mubarak had been battling the flu while observing the traditional daytime fast during the Muslim holy month of Ramadan. It was packaged for public consumption as yet another example of Mubarak's piety and selfless dedication to his sacred duties, even in the face of physical hardships.

On the day of Mubarak's collapse, I was riding a microbus when the news broke. My fellow passengers began openly speculating about a post-Mubarak Egypt, who should take over after him, and whether Gamal Mubarak was really being groomed for the job. One man spoke up and said he actually hoped that the presidency would stay in the Mubarak family. His reasoning was a classic example of Egyptian world-weary cynicism.

"At least [the Mubaraks] have been stealing from the country for twenty years. They're probably satisfied," the man said. "If somebody new comes in, they're going to come in hungry."

In the summer of 2004, a new entity emerged on the opposition scene: a movement called Kefaya or "Enough." Mostly composed of like-minded leftists, Kefaya built itself around one overarching goal: preventing Gamal Mubarak from succeeding his father.

In the preceding years, the Gamal presidential grooming campaign had moved from rumor-fueled conspiracy theory to extremely realistic possibility. It started slowly at first; Gamal would mysteriously begin appearing at his father's side in the newspaper photos and television footage. Often the captions and television presenters wouldn't even note his presence. Compared to Syria, where the Parliament in 2000 literally rewrote the constitutional age requirement overnight in order to install Bashar Al-Assad, Gamal Mubarak's introduction to public life was conducted with remarkable and uncharacteristic subtlety.

He started attending high-level meetings, even accompanying senior ministers on trips to Washington, D.C., to meet with American officials. He gave interviews to CNN in fluent English, frequently denying that he had any presidential ambitions. By 2004, he had emerged as a force within the ruling National Democratic Party and was being publicly packaged as a young reformer bringing new ideas.

There was a growing air of inevitability about him. Gamal began easing out some of his father's more old-school lieutenants in favor of his own clique. Crucially, the Americans seemed to be on board as well, already treating him like a vital part of the Egyptian government. (Once during a high-level Egyptian ministerial junket to Washington, I spent a fruitless day on the phone trying to get various U.S. government spokesmen to explain to me why Gamal Mubarak—who held no actual elected or even appointed government position—was sitting in a room with American congressmen and cabinet members.)

Really the only potential roadblocks to a Gamal presidency were whether the military would accept a civilian ruler and whether his father was willing to give up power to anyone, no less his son. Kassem, the publisher and close observer of Egyptian politics, always insisted during this period that Gamal Mubarak would never become president—but only because he believed the generals would reject him. At no point in years of Gamal speculation was the prospect of the citizens of the country rebelling against hereditary succession considered to be a serious possibility.

The Kefaya movement sought to throw a wrench into that momentum. With brilliant branding and iconic yellow stickers proclaiming its one-word slogan, the group launched a series of memorable protests in 2004 and 2005. The international media fell in love, inflating the name to heights that its actual numbers and support never justified. Then a year later, when the movement had failed to truly connect with the wider Egyptian population, those same correspondents pronounced the movement a fizzle.

In retrospect, Kefaya deserves to be remembered as more than an interesting and feisty failure. The group played a major role in setting the stage for future events. A new generation of young leftists essentially came of age politically under the Kefaya banner and remained politically active afterward. And more than any other movement, Kefaya shattered the mystique around the Mubarak name; they were the first to focus their chants directly against the dictator himself. It also helped solidify the trend started a year earlier in the Iraq war protests—refocusing the anger of activists away from foreign policy side alleys and directly on the country's domestic situation.

The first time I observed a Kefaya demonstration, outside the presidential palace in Abdin on a broiling hot summer day, it was shocking and a little scary to hear the Mubarak name so loudly taken in vain. In the years that followed, the anti-Mubarak chants would become a routine part of opposition politics; but Kefaya changed the game in a crucial and permanent way.

The years 2004 and 2005 also represented a watershed moment for U.S.-Egyptian relations, one with serious domestic repercussions. In the wake of the World Trade Center attacks of September 11, 2001, the government of President George W. Bush launched a short-lived campaign to truly press for democratic reform in longtime Arab allies like Egypt, arguing that repressive domestic systems helped lay the seeds for Islamic fundamentalism.

Egyptians, regardless of educational levels or literacy rates, are an extremely politically savvy population. They had heard Washington rhetoric about democratization before; but this time the Americans actually seemed to mean it, and the Egyptians took notice.

After months of public and private pressure, Mubarak

responded by pushing through a constitutional amendment that instituted Egypt's first-ever multicandidate
presidential elections. It was hailed locally as Mubarak's
latest tremendous and benevolent gift to the nation, but
the Americans were not placated. A month after the
amendment passed, Secretary of State Condoleezza Rice
came to Cairo and basically embarrassed the Mubarak
regime on its own home turf. In a watershed moment on
June 20, 2005, Rice delivered a historically harsh speech
on campus at the American University in Cairo. Refer-
encing parliamentary elections coming up that fall, Rice
basically ordered Cairo to play fair, lift the emergency
laws, give the opposition a chance, permit international monitoring, and generally speaking, behave itself
for once.

"The Egyptian government must put its faith in its
own people," she said. "The day must come when the rule
of law replaces emergency decrees and when the independent judiciary replaces arbitrary justice. The Egyptian government must fulfill the promise it has made to
its people and to the entire world by giving its citizens
the freedom to choose."

Bush and Rice probably won't be remembered too
fondly in Egyptian history; the Iraq invasion was almost
universally viewed here as naked petro-imperialism
using 9-11 as a pretext.

But this brief window—when America abandoned re-
gional realpolitik—deserves to be remembered generously.
Rice's Cairo speech was littered with political firebombs.
In comparison to normally obtuse diplo-speak, this was

more than a shot across the bow; it was a punch to the gut. No U.S. diplomat in generations had talked to Egypt like this, and none ever has since. In contrast, President Barack Obama's much-hyped Cairo speech of June 2009 sounds flaccid.

Egypt, Rice said, "must meet objective standards that define every free election," and added, "It is time to abandon the excuses that are made to avoid the hard work of democracy."

Most important, the Bush administration's public statements were backed by private pressure as well. Mubarak was able to fend off calls for international election monitors, but Egypt's perennially inconvenient judges had already inserted themselves into that situation, ruling that *they* would personally serve as polling place monitors for the parliamentary elections that fall.

Mubarak easily won re-election on September 7, 2005, running against actual human beings for the first time ever. His main challenger, Ayman Nour of the Ghad (Tomorrow) Party captured somewhere between 7 and 12 percent of the vote, depending on whose figures you believe. Nour, a longtime opposition parliamentarian, had already been in and out of jail that year on charges he had forged signatures on the Ghad Party's application for government approval. A month after the presidential vote, he was sentenced to five years in prison. Nour became a rallying point and an enduring sore spot in U.S.-Egyptian relations. But he was never a serious threat to Mubarak's reign. Still, the sight of Nour (or anyone really) aggressively criticizing and running against Mubarak played a lasting psychological role—like Kefaya, it was another step in chipping away at the mystique.

The presidential vote was merely a place setter for the real battleground: parliamentary elections. The vote was held in three stages over the course of a month, in order to ensure that a judge was installed inside all polling stations around the country. With the Americans watching closely from the outside, and the judges watching from the inside, the regime was effectively cornered. The only ploy available to the government was to violently control the streets around the polling stations.

"You couldn't fake things on the inside. So what would they do? State Security simply told its troops to prevent the 'wrong kind' of voters from even approaching the polling places," said police Gen. Ahmed Khalil. "Anyone known to be attached to opposition politics or anyone who even looked like an Islamist couldn't get near the building."

These tactics only served to partially limit the extent of the disaster. In terms of sheer numbers, the NDP maintained a dominating hold on Parliament, with nearly 70 percent of the 454 seats. But the elections proved two things: the grassroots power of the venerable Islamist opposition group, the Muslim Brotherhood, and the complete public abandonment of the officially licensed and tamed pseudo-opposition parties.

Founded in Egypt in 1928, the Brotherhood had mushroomed into a border-spanning umbrella organization that pioneered the cause of political Islam and heavily influenced younger groups like Hamas and Hizbullah.

Under Mubarak the Brotherhood had a curious existence; operating semi-openly but still formally banned from public life and subject to routine mass crackdowns. Simply being a member was a jailable offense, but at the same time the group maintained the same office in Cairo's Manial district for years with an actual sign on the door reading "Muslim Brotherhood."

Banned from forming an official political party, the Brotherhood candidates in 2005 instead ran as nominal independents under the unifying campaign slogan, "Islam is the solution." Brotherhood affiliated MPs captured eighty-eight seats—20 percent of the Parliament—and immediately became the legislature's largest opposition bloc. Official opposition parties like the Wafd—who needed government permission to exist in the first place—performed terribly. No single opposition party captured more than six seats. As much as proving the Brotherhood's deserved place in the Egyptian political arena, the election proved that nobody was looking to the licensed opposition to provide actual political opposition to the government. Secular-minded opponents of the regime either cast protest votes for the Brotherhood or sat out the process altogether. It was a sentiment that, a few years later, Mohammed ElBaradei would successfully tap into—arguing that the licensed opposition and the government were all part of the same system and true change could only come from outside that framework.

The Bush Administration's Middle East domestic reform campaign wouldn't last much longer. A few weeks after the Muslim Brotherhood's parliamentary triumphs, the Palestinian militant group Hamas dominated parliamentary elections there, embarrassing the United States and Israeli-backed Fatah faction. The twin Islamist democratic victories were enough to scare the Americans off their campaign. Democracy was a fine and noble concept, as long as it didn't produce a government of scary bearded Muslims in power. From that point on, the United States settled back into its old, time-worn and halfhearted rhetoric. But much like the Kefaya summer, the short-lived Bush democracy push represented yet another small but crucial point of no return.

Most foreign observers of the Egyptian revolution are familiar by now with the April 6 Movement, one of an intertwined collection of social media-savvy youth movements that helped provide that final organizational push toward revolution. But it seems likely that a certain percentage of those observers are unaware of the events that gave the movement its name.

On April 6, 2008, workers at Egypt's largest textile factory in the Nile Delta city of Mahalla al-Kubra engaged riot police in two days of violent clashes. It was the culmination of years of simmering labor unrest around the country, fueled by a rising cost of living, stagnant salaries, and an economic liberalization program that many laborers felt was a final betrayal of Nasser's socialist visions. *Al-Masry Al-Youm*, the country's largest independently owned newspaper, estimated that between 2004 and 2008, Egypt witnessed more than nineteen hundred separate labor actions involving 1.7 million workers.

The larger dynamic was the government's ongoing push to reshape the economy by privatizing hundreds of state-owned industries. While generally lauded by the IMF and World Bank as necessary steps toward modernizing Egypt's economy, the process provoked escalating suspicion and hostility among Egyptian workers. Critics charged that state institutions were being sold in nontransparent backroom deals for a fraction of their true values and workers' rights were being ignored in the process. In one notorious case, the Amonsito textile factory, employing twelve hundred workers, was sold to a Syrian businessman, who, facing a stack of bad debts and a looming prison sentence, ended up fleeing the country. In 2006 the Omar Effendi chain of department stores, a longstanding cultural icon akin to a Sears or Macy's, was sold to a Saudi investor for just over LE500 million—about $90 million. Former Omar Effendi board members complained loudly at the time that the chain's true value was close to double that amount. Other private sector investors provoked public fury by simply behaving like responsible capitalists—inheriting bloated overstaffed industries and trimming costs by laying off redundant or incompetent workers.

In June 2010, I interviewed Minister of Investment Mahmoud Mohieldin, one of the main architects of the privatization program. Mohieldin, who departed for a senior position at the World Bank three months later, acknowledged that there was a significant "social cost" that inevitably came with any privatization push.

"Even in some of the developed capitalist countries, the issue of privatization was never popular. I didn't really see any demonstrations with people raising banners or wearing T-shirts that say 'I love privatization' or 'I love Mrs. Thatcher' because of what she did in the UK," Mohieldin told me. "It's a very hard policy you need to deal with to face big problems. You are solving problems of inefficiency, incompetence, burdens on the budget which are not very much understood or even appreciated by many people."

The minister said some of the public companies being sold off were overstaffed by as much as 40 percent, calling the phenomenon, "a kind of disguised unemployment. So what to do about that? Basically you have to downsize. Nobody likes to see anybody made redundant, and those who are being made redundant are not responsible for being employed by a mistake or by political interference."

The Mahalla dispute wasn't actually a privatization issue; the twenty-seven thousand workers at the state-owned Misr Spinning and Weaving Company had been protesting for two years for better working conditions and higher wages to match the rising costs of living. On April 6, 2008, a preannounced plan to strike on the factory floor was preempted by security agents, who essentially occupied the factory. But later that afternoon, police attempts to break up groups of workers gathering outside the plant turned extremely violent on both sides. The clashes left two dead and dozens injured amid charges that security forces had used stun guns and live ammunition.

Mahalla served as a long-awaited clarion call to the country's once-robust socialist forces—proof that years of quiet grassroots development in the working class provinces were starting to bear dramatic fruit. Movements like Kefaya had made waves and broken political barriers, but had ultimately failed to develop into more than Cairo- and Alexandria-based middle-class phenomena. Mahalla and dozens of other parallel strikes served to finally fuse the country's political and democratic grievances with its economic grievances.

The government seemed to know immediately just how dangerous an issue it had on its hands. The Al Jazeera satellite news channels had covered the Mahalla clashes and filmed dramatic footage of workers there tearing down a huge poster of Mubarak. Jazeera International Correspondent Rawya Rageh recalls practically smuggling the tape back into Cairo and transmitting it to her newsroom in Qatar. The network ran the footage in heavy rotation for a day, and the Egyptian government immediately went ballistic, threatening Jazeera at the highest levels and even shutting down, on a trumped up licensing charge, the video production company that provided the satellite uplink. The issue became so radioactive that Jazeera basically locked the Mahalla footage away in a vault for years.

The Mahalla al-Kubra clashes moved Egypt's domestic economic grievances onto the national front burner and helped kick off a wave of labor organization and activity that never really stopped, even after the revolution. Suddenly there seemed to be a dozen new strikes each month, ranging from factory workers and bus drivers to doctors. In many cases the workers were rebelling against not only their immediate bosses, but against their own government-appointed "labor leaders"—part of a network of official trade unions that barely made a pretense of representing the actual workers. In one hilarious example, the government's own tax collectors became one of the templates for the resurgent labor movement, repeatedly striking and eventually forming their own independent wildcat union in December 2008. From April 6 onward, issues like the establishment of a LE1200 (just over $200) per month minimum wage became core demands alongside democratic issues like the repeal of the emergency laws.

As Mubarak's apparatus grew weaker, the societal forces arrayed against him grew stronger. All through the first decade of the twenty-first century, things were consistently bubbling along the edges. New NGOs were springing up, each causing a little bit of trouble. Online activists were multiplying and finding each other. But in the larger nonpoliticized culture, a palpable sense of despair and helplessness was taking hold. Perhaps most disturbing, the moral rot at the top had started to seep noticeably

LIBERATION SQUARE

through society in a sort of sinister trickle-down effect. Egypt, always rightfully known for the enduring sweetness and big-heartedness of its people, became a harsher and more cutthroat place. As the citizens internalized the realities of a society with almost no reliable and uncorrupted institutions, Egyptians began to genuinely forget about the concept of right and wrong, or justice under the law. All disputes, large or small, immediately devolved into power games and battles of competing *wusta*—influence or connections.

"Mubarak destroyed Egypt. He destroyed the morals and the conscience of the people," said Maha Elgamal, a wealthy homemaker and businesswoman, who spent much of 2010 gathering signatures for Mohammed El-Baradei's campaign for sweeping domestic reform. "It's not even a matter of what they stole. It's the effect they had on the culture of the people. I feel like we have to raise new human beings from scratch."

I recall a long conversation with a friend named Khaled during a visit to Cairo somewhere in 2008—I was, at the time, living in Jerusalem as a correspondent with the *Los Angeles Times*. Khaled had just been through a painful breakup with his fiancée and wanted the return of jewelry and other gifts he had given her. The striking and dispiriting thing about Khaled's account was that at no point in the dispute was any thought given to finding a legitimate and trusted societal arbitrator, such as a small claims court. Instead, the entire standoff moved instantly into a sort of *wusta* chess match. "She has an uncle who was a police general," Khaled told me, "but I have a close friend

56

who is a senior officer in the Presidential Guards." Khaled seemed confident that his *wusta* would trump her *wusta*. Nothing else mattered.

The sheer claustrophobic desperation and widespread moral decay of these final Mubarak years seeped out into the public consciousness in multiple forms. One of these escape valves was popular cinema—where mixed in among the steady parade of noisy escapist slapstick comedies, there remained an undercurrent of films expressing the unmistakable laments of a society approaching its nadir. In these movies, it's not always the government trapping and oppressing these people. It's just as often larger societal issues, mindless bureaucracy, class barriers, and ground-level interpersonal exploitation. There's a small stack of films from the late-Mubarak period that offer this kind of window into the national psyche, but two of them are especially indicative. Both movies, while different in tone, approach, and depth, are essentially taking bites of the same thematic apple. Egypt, in the last decade of the Mubarak era, lost something important—several things actually. Hope, confidence, dignity, self-sufficiency, optimism for the future, a sense of community and basic interpersonal decency—all of these traits began to be viewed as hallmarks of a bygone era. Everyone seemed to know that one of the world's oldest and proudest civilizations was rapidly sliding backward.

Cultural Film (2000) disguises itself as a slapstick farce about libidinous youth, akin to the *American Pie* franchise; it is, in fact, one of the saddest portraits of young Egyptian despair ever created. The name comes

from one of the local euphemisms for pornography—
during the annual Cairo International Film Festival,
downtown theater owners used to advertise a "cultural
film" as a thinly coded siren call to young men that whatever European import was being screened inside featured nudity.

The movie centers on three friends—Effat, Ashraf, and
Alaa. All are in their late twenties and completely adrift.
Effat is still in college, and can't concentrate on his studies because of all the attractive women surrounding him.
The other two have long-since graduated, and are jobless
and basically consumed with thoughts of sex. Ashraf
wakes up extra early just to leer at the neighbor across the
alley hanging up laundry in her nightgown; Alaa spends
his nights intensely inspecting a women's fashion magazine with a magnifying glass.

It's all played for laughs, but the sociology is never far
from the surface. Early in the movie, Alaa's mother comes
to wake him and his college-age brother. The brother
moans that there's no point in going to college anyway.

"What am I going to do with a degree," he complains,
gesturing to the lump in the next bed. "My older brother
is all educated and graduated seven years ago and there
he is."

That's essentially the film's message. There are no jobs
out there—at least none that pay enough for these young
men to ever be able to save enough for their own apartment. No savings and no apartment means living at home
with their parents in a state of permanent, infantilized

arrested development. More immediately, it means no hope of ever having sex.

This is actually a very real societal problem in Egypt. Housing prices have spiraled exponentially, especially in the overcrowded capital, while salaries for all but a privileged few remain flat. The end result is that the concept of "an apartment" has become something very nearly sacred and mythical in Egyptian society. Having an apartment is the key to actually starting the adult portion of your life.

But Egyptians very rarely rent to other Egyptians for a variety of reasons—including societal suspicion of someone who isn't living at home, and a fear that with the nonexistent state of law enforcement, it will be impossible to evict delinquent tenants. And proper long-term mortgage loans don't really exist, which means that buying an apartment means putting up a massive chunk of money in advance.

As a result, even those young couples who manage to navigate the treacherous waters of romance and find each other often spend the next decade-plus in a state of permanent engagement, saving up for that apartment as well as for equally expensive furnishings and appliances.

All along the Nile, you can find patches of green space overlooking the water that serve as a sort of chaste Muslim-world version of a lover's lane. On any given night you can stroll past and find multiple young couples sitting with each other, drinking soda and eating sandwiches. With every penny going toward savings for the apartment, this is the cheapest possible night out. The couples cluster together, often sitting as close to each other as law and society allow; sexual tension (both male and female) crackles through the air like an electric current.

Often these are college sweethearts who won't be able to get married until they are well into their thirties. Just as often, the pressures and stresses of this waiting period drive them apart. It's an under-explored issue just how much pure sexual frustration fed into Egypt's revolutionary rage.

With nothing better to do, the three friends in *Cultural Film* spend their time in a local coffee shop, smoking shisha pipes. Their primary activity—really the focus of their entire lives—seems to revolve around securing access to pornography (keep in mind this film is set a few years before the Internet really took hold in Egypt). They hear through the apparently robust sexually-frustrated-youth-grapevine that an acquaintance is in possession of an X-rated movie. The entire rest of the film is a starstruck quest for a sort of holy trinity for sexually frustrated Egyptian youth: the tape itself, an empty apartment to watch it in, and a VCR.

It never works, of course. The obstacles are too daunting, and through an endless and implausible set of twists and turns, the trio is foiled in every attempt. With each new failure, the young men's palpable frustration and anxiety rises. At one point, a despairing Effat yells, "How many like us are out there? We're supposed to just go to hell and shut up and forget all talk of love or marriage, and thank God that cultural films exist so we can at least pretend."

But rather than portray them as mere pathetic perverts, the film casts its three protagonists as emblems of their generation. As the plot progresses, more and more young men join the cause as soon as they hear the trio has an actual porno in hand. By the end there are more than a dozen guys crisscrossing the city together searching for an empty place with some privacy so they can watch their movie.

Perhaps the clearest sign that *Cultural Film* was delving into some seriously powerful sociology is its ending. After spending nearly two hours depicting just how trapped and hopeless the young men are, the movie struggles to wrap up with honesty. Back at the coffee shop, Effat suddenly gets inspired and announces he's determined to leave the porn behind and "take a stand in life"—whatever that means. As the three suddenly optimistic friends are walking down the street, they're nearly run over by a car. Out of the vehicle steps Yousra—a huge glamorous film star making a brief cameo as herself. She chats with the boys a bit, gives them a free copy of her latest movie, and drives off. The friends laugh uproariously in the street as the credits roll.

It's a cop-out, but also an understandable choice by the filmmakers. After all, these young men not only have very little hope of ever getting married or having sex, they can't even find a place to masturbate in peace. If the movie really wanted to track events through to a logical conclusion, these three friends would have no true options other than to start a revolution, join a fundamentalist cell, or kill themselves.

When Alaa Al Aswany published his second novel, *The Yacoubian Building,* in 2002, it was an immediate social phenomenon—both for its lurid depictions of the capital's seedy underbelly and its mercilessly accurate exploration of the hypocrisy, corruption, hopelessness, and all-around moral rot that came to characterize modern Egypt.

The book was the bestselling novel in the Arab world for several years in a row; it was eventually translated into English and made into a major 2006 studio film starring a host of prominent Egyptian actors. The title refers to a grand old building in downtown Cairo. A large cast of intertwining characters revolve around the building— either wealthy residents or impoverished dwellers of a virtual shantytown that has been created on the roof.

The characters include Zaki Dessouki, a rich engineer who spends most of his energy pursuing women; Hagg Muhammed Azzam, a self-made millionaire who owns a chain of department stores; Hatim Rachid, a cultured aristocrat who edits a government-run French-language newspaper and who barely bothers to hide his homosexuality; Taha El Shazli, the son of the building's *bowab*—a sort of live-in doorman and security guard; and Buthayna El Sayed, an impoverished young woman living with her family in a cramped tin shack on the building's roof.

Taha, the *bowab*'s son, is intelligent and motivated, dreaming of becoming a police officer. His ambitions are dashed by Egypt's cruelly rigid class barriers. Regardless of his qualifications, his interview at the police academy ends as soon as the officers there realize he is a mere *bowab*'s son. Buthayna, whose father died young leaving the family in debt, is forced into the job market to support her siblings. When she quits a job because of constant sexual advances from the boss, her own mother rebukes her for her selfishness. A friend helps her secure another job in a clothing store and advises Buthayna to wise up and stop being so high-minded about her honor. Sure enough, the new boss aggressively gropes her at the first opportunity, and a broken Buthayna lets it happen. Buthayna and Taha are childhood sweethearts, but their relationship crumbles amid Taha's frustration at his lack of options in life and Buthayna's hardening cynicism about the way the world really works.

Hagg Azzam, wealthy, comfortable, and respected, experiences a bit of a midlife crisis and wants to seek sex outside his marriage. He's advised by a wonderfully cynical Muslim sheikh who can find a Quranic verse to justify just about anything. Under Islam, Hagg Azzam could legitimately take a second wife but he fears public scandal (and his first wife's fury), so he and his trusty sheikh devise an alternative plan. The secretary of a business acquaintance in Alexandria catches his eye—Souad is a widow in her late thirties—and he makes her a deeply cynical offer. In exchange for what amounts to a generous monthly salary, she will leave her son behind in

Alexandria and Azzam will set her up in a Cairo apartment. The pair will be "married" in secret with the sheikh's blessing. It's one step removed from prostitution, disguised in layers of piety and religious hypocrisy.

The Yacoubian Building depicts a world that is rapidly running short on common morality. Out of about a dozen primary characters, there seem to be three decent human beings—Taha, Buthayna, and Souad—and they generally spend the narrative being exploited, physically abused, disillusioned, and driven half-crazy. The rich exploit the poor, the poor exploit each other just as badly, and occasionally one of the poor manages to exploit one of the rich—like when a lower-class waitress that Zaki Dessouki is trying to seduce ends up drugging his drink and robbing him. The police turn up frequently throughout the narrative, but never in a positive light. They're either arresting and torturing peaceful activists or being used as a tool in somebody's power games—a weapon that those with money and influence use to threaten those lower on the societal food chain.

Even the semi-sympathetic characters like Hatim, the gay newspaper editor, are far from heroic. Hatim seems to have no interest in dating other gay men of his social standing, focusing instead on impoverished police officers from the countryside with whom he can play sugar daddy. Zaki Dessouki, the most prominent character, is generally well meaning. But he's a dilettante—educated, urbane, and privileged, he makes no attempt to contribute anything to society or even to perform an honest day's labor.

Taha, the *bowab*'s frustrated son, eventually drifts into

a militant Islamist group, seeking some sort of justice and order in his world. He is arrested and viciously tortured by the police officers whose ranks he once hoped to join. Eventually he flees to a rural militant training camp, returning to Cairo to launch a suicidal revenge mission against his torturers. Hatim, the newspaper editor, embarks on a doomed "romance" with a simple police conscript named Abduh. The soldier has a wife and child back in his village, and doesn't even seem to be gay; but he is grateful to have a benefactor. When he finally tries to break free from Hatim, the wealthy man threatens to use his police connections to get Abduh arrested on a trumped-up robbery charge, so Abduh snaps and beats him to death.

Azzam decides to cement his success by running for Parliament—or really buying his way into the corridors of power. He meets with a powerful regime fixer named Kamal al-Fouli—a very thinly veiled caricature of a real-life Mubarak minister and power broker named Kamal El Shazli who died in 2010. Al-Fouli blatantly lays out how much it will cost to buy a seat, making it clear the ruling party can install in or oust from the Parliament anyone they want. Meanwhile, Azzam's secret wife Souad is becoming a problem. She discovers she is pregnant and wants to keep the baby. At one point Azzam brings along his trusty sheikh, who spouts Quranic verses to somehow justify an abortion—absolutely forbidden in Islam unless the mother's life is in danger. Azzam resorts to violence; Souad is attacked in her apartment by unknown assailants. She wakes up in the hospital and is informed by the doctors that she had a miscarriage.

Azzam's deal with the ruling party devil also turns problematic. Once he's on the hook, al-Fouli, the government power broker, cheerfully explains that he now owes the government 25 percent of all future earnings. When Azzam balks, he is dramatically put in his place.

This is the only major plot point where the movie diverges substantially from the book, and the discrepancy speaks volumes. In the novel, Azzam is summoned to an appointment with "the Big Man." His name is never mentioned and his face is never shown, but this can only be President Hosni Mubarak. Hagg Azzam never actually meets the Big Man; inside the presidential palace, he is shown into an empty room. The Big Man speaks to him through a loudspeaker and roughly tells Azzam that the State Security file on the table reveals the truth: behind his pious façade, Azzam is one of the country's largest heroin importers. Of course, the government doesn't want to arrest or expose him, they just want their cut.

In the movie, there's the same basic scenario. Azzam balks at the government's escalating demands and has to be intimidated into complying. But on film there's no reference to a Big Man. Instead, one of Azzam's car dealerships is suddenly subjected to a massive raid by the Interior Ministry's narcotics squad. As the officers begin to search the dealership, Azzam is forced to call al-Fouli and surrender to the government's conditions.

It's no surprise that the Mubarak inference is cut from the movie. If anything, it's surprising that Al Aswany got away with putting it in his book.

The tale ends on something of a high note. Zaki Dessouki and Buthayna embark on an improbable romance and are married, in defiance of massive differences in their ages and social standings. But like *Cultural Film,* this abrupt turn into optimism seems a little jarring given the unrelenting darkness and venality that precedes it.

It's a thoroughly depressing story; more than any other work of modern Egyptian popular fiction, *The Yacoubian Building* paints the portrait of Egypt as a country and a society that absolutely *needed* to have a revolution.

4

The Emergency Law Martyr

By all accounts, Khaled Saieed was just about the least likely candidate in Egypt to become a revolutionary rallying point, much less the face that helped bring down a regime. According to his own close friends, the twenty-eight-year-old Alexandrian was a bit of an oddball—introverted, shy, sensitive to the point of emotional fragility, and a bit of a recluse. He liked strumming the guitar, playing with his cats, and remixing rap and techno music on his computer.

"All his life he was sitting at home with his computer and his music," said Haitham Mesbah, a close friend of Khaled's and a witness to his final violent and terrified moments at the hands of a pair of plainclothes Egyptian police officers. "He wouldn't leave the house except to get food or new things for his computer. We would go a month without seeing him. If you wanted to see him, you went to his house."

He wasn't a shut-in or antisocial by any means. Guests were always welcome to stop by. Khaled's father died when he was young and his mother Leila split her time living between Alexandria and his sister's home in Cairo, so Khaled was living alone much of the time. Posthumous articles invariably identified Saieed as a "young Alexandria businessman," which is overstating his economic status; in truth the closest thing Saieed had to a business was a small-time trade selling stereo equipment that his brother would ship him from America.

In his mid-twenties, Khaled started serving his mandatory time in the Egyptian military, but he quickly proved to be not cut out for the rigors of army life. Within a few months, according to Haitham Mesbah, Khaled basically went AWOL while on weekend leave. He stayed out for at least two years, keeping a low profile in his neighborhood, but nobody really seemed to be looking for him. Khaled's plan, Haitham said, was to stay off the radar until age thirty, then surrender himself and pay a sizable fine—a customary loophole for middle-class families that can afford it. Eventually Khaled returned to the military voluntarily; he dreamed of traveling to the United States and needed proof of military service on his passport in order to leave the country.

Like a healthy percentage of Egyptian youth (and adults for that matter) Khaled enjoyed the occasional puff of hashish, but didn't seem to be a heavier-than-usual consumer. In the winter, when Alexandria's summer tourist traffic thinned, Khaled, Haitham, and other friends like Kareem Samir would rent out a beach cabin along the Mediterranean, bringing along Khaled's huge stereo system and spend hours playing Estimation—a locally popular variation of the card game Spades.

"He was sweet and calm and childlike," said Kareem Samir, a recent law school graduate. "He would say that he really wanted to be famous. Well, it happened."

Saieed will be remembered as Egypt's Mohammed Bouazizi—a tragic and seemingly run-of-the-mill case that somehow lights the fuse. Bouazizi essentially incited the whole Arab Spring single-handledly; the young Tunisian fruit-seller's public suicide in December 2010 sparked his country's revolution, and everything that followed. The sheer despair in Bouazizi's gesture captured his countrymen's imaginations and evoked their long simmering frustrations. Khaled Saieed's death in a dim Alexandria doorway did much the same in Egypt. The comparison is, of course, a little imperfect. Bouazizi's death touched off an immediate inferno, while the Egyptians simply added Khaled's case to their stew of bubbling grievances.

Still, Saieed's death angered people in a deeper-than-usual way. It also marked the beginning of a sustained escalation in protest activity that didn't let up until the revolution. His name became a touchstone, symbolic of the decades-long excesses of the Egyptian police state under the emergency laws—an instant shorthand for the arbitrary nature of the brutality in the late-stage Mubarak era.

"That didn't just piss people off. It scared them as well. The 'That could happen to me' effect really was very specific to Khaled, and not to other police brutality cases," said Mohamed El Dahshan, an international development specialist and activist who blogs under the name "Traveler Within." "He was super middle-class, the archetypal young Egyptian. He kind of looks like you, or if not you then your brother. His mother looks like your mother."

On June 6, 2010, at about eleven o'clock at night, about a month after the Parliament had voted to renew the emergency laws for two more years, Khaled stopped into the Space Net Cybercafé just down the street from his apartment in Alexandria's seaside Cleopatra district. It was a typical summer night and the street was throbbing with activity, with multiple coffee shops and shisha cafés working, juice shops selling everything from banana milkshakes to fresh-pressed sugar cane juice. Alexandria is generally sleepy in the winter but hums with a late-night vibe all summer, and the clothing and computer stores on Boubaset Street stay open well past midnight.[2]

Khaled wasn't a regular at Space Net; he preferred working on his own computer at home. But he had a lot of friends who gathered there. Spotting one of these acquaintances playing PlayStation Soccer, Khaled entered to say hello. He never made it. Within seconds, two plainclothes police officers—Mahmoud Salah Mahmoud and Awad Ismael Suleiman—entered Space Net, one through

---

2 One year after Khaled's death, I visited Boubaset Street around the same time of night as the incident. It was immediately clear from the level of street activity that there would have been *a lot* of witnesses.

the front entrance and the other from a nearby side door that leads to an alley, and made a direct line for Khaled. He liked to wear his hair longish in the back and one of the officers grabbed a handful.

"It was immediate. He didn't even get to say a word to his friend," said Hassan Mesbah, the owner of Space Net, whose son Haitham was a close friend of Khaled's. "I heard the fuss and came down and saw two people grabbing a guy by the back of his neck."

Visitors to Space Net enter a narrow corridor leading to a small set of stairs. On the left is a chest-high marble shelf with barstools for customers who bring their own laptops and use the Space Net Wi-Fi. Past that is an alcove with a collection of couches and a huge television hooked to a PlayStation. Up the stairs are Mesbah's desk and then two rooms with clusters of multiple computer terminals.

When Hassan Mesbah responded to the sudden commotion, he saw his son Haitham already arguing with the officers. Khaled shouted, "What do you want? Don't grab me like this!" One of the officers slammed Khaled's head hard into the nearby marble counter.

Hassan shouted at the men to take their dispute outside, so they dragged the struggling Saieed into the foyer of an apartment building two doors down, pausing to bang his head into the metal doorway. Mohammed Naieem, the building's *bowab*, witnessed the ensuing beating, saying the two officers spent twenty minutes kicking Saieed and slamming his head into the concrete floor as he pleaded for mercy.

"It wasn't a normal beating. It was a lethal attack," Naieem told me.

At one point, Khaled yelled out, "I'm going to die!" The remorseless response: "Either way, you're dead."

In the meantime, a crowd had formed in the street outside. When neighbors tried to get involved, one of the officers shouted, "Anyone who interferes will go in his place."

One man shouted at the police, "You oppressors, you sons of bitches!" But according to Hassan Mesbah, another resident counseled the crowd to mind their own business, saying, "Leave [the police] to their work."

Eventually Khaled went limp, but the beating continued, the officers seemingly in denial about how much damage they were doing. Finally Naieem told the officers, "He's dead," but they responded, "He's not dead. Nobody say that."

One of the coffee shop patrons across the street was a local physician and he approached the scene and managed to quickly inspect the body, and told them, "Enough! You're beating a dead man."

One of the officers told him, "No, he's faking it. We'll wake him up now," and the physician responded, "I'm a doctor and I'm telling you he's dead."

After a while, the officers seemed to finally realize the truth, touching off a chaotic and revealing series of damage-control steps. One of them made a phone call; Haitham Mesbah said he heard him say, "Sir we have an issue here." Within ten minutes a senior police officer arrived, and the three of them loaded Khaled's body into the officer's car.

"They took the body and left," Hassan Mesbah said. "Ten minutes later, they came back with what seemed like dozens of cars and officers and tossed the body back into the same stairwell."

"They tossed him like a sack of garbage," said Hassan's son Haitham.

By now it was well past midnight. With the neighborhood swarming with police and with residents enraged over what they had witnessed, an ambulance was summoned. While waiting for the ambulance to arrive, the police bizarrely propped Saieed's lifeless body in a sitting position against the wall, "like they were pretending he was still alive," Naieem said.

When the ambulance arrived, the driver at first refused to transport the body—correctly stating that corpse removal was the legally mandated job of the coroner's office.

"He's dead, I can't take him," the driver said, according to Haitham Mesbah, who witnessed the exchange. The senior officer on the scene essentially bullied him into compliance, saying, "No, you're taking him. Let's get this over with."

At about three o'clock in the morning, Saieed's family was summoned to the morgue to identify the body. One relative surreptitiously took a cell-phone camera photo that will live forever in Egyptian history.

The photo is horrific. Khaled's face is cut and mangled, several teeth seem to be missing and blood is still pooling underneath his head. The picture exploded onto the Egyptian Internet, along with a parallel image—a generic studio passport shot of a young Khaled, looking every inch the image of modern Egyptian youth: gelled hair, long sideburns, a bit of a soul patch under his bottom lip, and a gray hooded sweatshirt.

"The huge thing with Khaled Saieed wasn't his picture after he got killed. It was his picture before he got killed. A little innocent-looking guy who looks like your son, your cousin, your nephew. That's what galvanized people," said Mahmoud Salem, aka Sandmonkey—one of the godfathers of the Egyptian blogosphere. "Khaled Saieed showed the middle class that their devil's bargain with the Ministry of Interior meant nothing. Being silent and minding their own business wouldn't protect them."

The visceral and deeply personal reaction to the incident reveals much about Egyptian society. After all, Khaled Saieed was hardly the first ordinary citizen tortured or even killed by the Security State. He wasn't the first such victim where hard and damning documentary evidence of the brutality existed, or even the first in the age of Facebook and Twitter as social organizing tools.

Much of the resonance of Khaled's death seems to center around Egypt's rigid class dynamics. Through monarchies and military republics, feudalism, socialism, and capitalism (in truth, probably dating back to the pharaohs) Egypt has always been a place with very little social mobility. The rich were rich and the poor were poor;

everyone stuck with their own reality and there were almost no ways to change that reality. Ironically, over the past seventy years or so, the army and police forces (along with the entertainment industry) have probably been the easiest way for a working class Egyptian to truly advance in society.

Bottom line: If it had been Mohammed Naieem, the *bowab* and witness, getting beaten to death that day, it wouldn't have made one tenth the impact. Three years earlier, activist bloggers circulated a video showing a twenty-one-year-old microbus driver named Emad al-Kebir being viciously sodomized with a stick in a police station. The case became a rallying point for activists and NGOs, causing enough of a fuss that the government was forced to sentence the two officers involved to three-year prison terms. But it basically ended there. Nobody formed a "We Are All Emad al-Kebir" Web site because they simply didn't feel that kind of instant kinship and sympathy.

"People could relate to that guy more than they could relate to some microbus driver," said Mohamed El Dahshan. "Before that, people could always brush [police brutality cases] off by saying 'Well, he must have done something to begin with if he was in the police station.'"

Much of what happened to Mubarak in February 2011 can be tied directly to what happened to Saieed in June 2010. It's fair to ask whether Mubarak would still be president today if he had simply gotten ahead of the issue and at least understood that his political self-interest demanded a robust response. What if Mubarak had recognized the depth and breadth of the popular anger on display, and ordered a proper investigation of the Saieed case, letting the chips fall where they may—even if that meant holding accountable senior officials of the Minister of Interior?

We'll never know because Mubarak either didn't realize or didn't care just how deep a nerve Saieed's death had struck. Instead citizens were treated to a routine cover-up and that seemed to enrage people all the more because of its dreary familiarity—just the latest in a long series of signs that the police dominance under the emergency law era would never be challenged or moderated.

Khaled's pictures and accompanying story went instantly viral, jumping from the online activist community to ordinary citizens within days. People began using his picture in the gray hooded sweatshirt as their Facebook avatars. Mahmoud Salem, the blogger, credits the country's social media community for essentially shoving the issue into the newspapers. As the independent press started to discover the story, witnesses like Hassan Mesbah spoke out and gave interviews detailing exactly what they had seen. Local and international human rights organizations rushed into the fray, demanding a proper investigation and a repeal of the emergency laws.

The ensuing furor touched off weeks of demonstrations around the country, many of which employed clever new tactics like flash-mob-style organization and live streaming videos of protests. In one memorable moment, activists organized a pair of silent vigils: at a prearranged time, participants wearing black stood in a long line on the Alexandria Corniche or along the Nile in Giza. There were no chants; they didn't even really interact with each other. Under the emergency laws, the police could pretty much declare all unauthorized protests or gatherings illegal. But there was no actual "protest" for the police to break up—just people standing at least five meters apart looking at the water, some of them reading the Quran or Bible.

"The final crescendo really started in June 2010," said Mohamed El Dahshan, the activist and blogger, who participated in the vigil. "One of the brilliant things about the Khaled Saieed movement is that they were very focused. They knew exactly what their issue was: police violence. They weren't talking about Gamal Mubarak or anything else."

This already simmering public anger spiked as the state's official cover story took shape. The ensuing police report made no mention of any kind of a beating and insisted that Saieed was a habitual criminal who choked to death on a packet of hashish he swallowed when he saw the officers approaching him. This version, of course, doesn't explain why Saieed's picture looks like he was run over by a truck. Amazingly, the ensuing coroner's report completely backed the police version. In response to continued and escalating protests, Saieed's body was exhumed and a second autopsy conducted. The second coroner's report came to the same conclusions as the first, adding speculation that his dramatic injuries were caused by "blunt objects" that he collided with "while trying to flee the police."

"They were adamant to defend their two officers," said

Kassem, the publisher and human right activist—and a native Alexandrian. "They could have thrown them to the wolves and finished it, but their policy was to defend everything."

In sweeping the Saieed issue under the rug, Mubarak's government helped hasten its own demise in a very real and tangible way. Existing organizations like the April 6 Movement immediately rallied around the issue, and entirely new movements were born from it.

A Facebook page under the name "We Are All Khaled Saieed" was created, and it became one of the main gathering points for organizers of the protests that eventually brought Mubarak down. The page's founder, Egyptian Google executive Wael Ghonim, became one of the iconic faces of the revolution.

Within a month, the regime was forced to reverse course and put the two officers, Mahmoud and Suleiman, on trial. In a belated attempt to get ahead of the story, Gamal Mubarak issued a statement claiming that the National Democratic Party "insists on the accountability of any wrongdoer within the framework of justice, transparency and the rule of law." He added that "respect for human rights and the fight against corruption" remained top NDP priorities.

But for many Egyptians the half-baked cover-up attempt was the last straw; suddenly fighting the regime wasn't just for agitators seeking trouble, it was necessary for everyone's survival. "What Khaled's case did was get people involved who didn't view what they were doing as politics," said Wael Khalil. "They saw it simply as doing the right thing."

The incident helped politicize untold numbers of Egyptians, touching a deep and powerful societal nerve and resonating among ordinary citizens who probably had never considered attending a demonstration before. People simply saw themselves, or their children, in Saieed's battered corpse. His death essentially became a nationwide referendum on the emergency laws and behavior of the police state under Mubarak. He was Egypt's "Emergency Law Martyr."

In late June 2010, about three weeks after his death, I attended a protest against police brutality in Saieed's name in Alexandria; immediately I could sense that something fundamental had shifted. This was larger, bolder, and angrier than usual, maybe three thousand strong and many of them claiming to be first-time attendees at *any* protest. When I pulled out my notebook and identified myself as a reporter, I was literally engulfed by people clamoring to tell me their own personal tales of injustice and mistreatment at the hands of the police. I could have written down a dozen examples, ranging from harassment and intimidation of political activists to Mafia-style shakedowns and casual everyday street corner humiliations.

"It's not just Khaled Saieed," said one Alexandrian law student who declined to give his name. "There have been hundreds of cases like this. It happens every day here."

Maha Ibrahim, a young Alexandria homemaker who wore the *niqab* (full face veil) made a point of having me write down her full name for publication and told me, "We're all afraid for our children. And we should be afraid because they are in danger. We're afraid of our own government."

Eighteen months later, in the midst of the revolution, I met a young woman named Amal in Tahrir Square. A young affluent mother, Amal admitted she had never cared about politics until the Khaled Saieed case.

"That really got to me. I have two boys and I felt he could be one of my sons," she told me. "That was a big turning point here."

One of the key unanswered questions about the Khaled Saieed case is why any of it happened in the first place. The eyewitness accounts make it clear this was no random beating. Khaled wasn't in the wrong place at the wrong time running across an officer in a pissy mood—a common enough circumstance that landed uncounted Egyptians in the crosshairs of the police state. That day, the two police officers were clearly waiting for him in ambush, one that was targeted and apparently very personal.

One of the dominant theories, circulated immediately after his death and based mostly on speculation from his family and friends, was that Khaled was being punished for posting a video on the Internet showing local police officers dividing up the spoils of a recent drug bust. It's a nice clean narrative, one that casts Khaled in the role of heroic crusader against corruption. But large chunks of the story simply don't add up.

The video is still freely available on YouTube under the headline, "This video is the reason the martyr Khaled Saieed was murdered," and it raises more questions than answers. It definitely depicts a group of senior police officers jovially congratulating each other in front of a desk loaded with large bricks of hashish. Bizarrely, they all seem aware they are being filmed by what appears to be a cell phone camera. The audio is extremely murky and it's hard to work out what people are saying. It has never been explained just why the officers allowed themselves to be filmed or how such potentially damning footage ended up in the hands of a small-timer like Saieed.

Haitham Mesbah, Khaled's close friend from the Space Net café, also casts doubt on this version of events. Khaled had absolutely no history of political activity, much less anything that would indicate he would be involved in exposing corruption in his local police force. Haitham insists that the video had been openly circulating in the Cleopatra district for weeks before Khaled's death. If Khaled had a copy on his computer's hard drive, it would be no surprise; Haitham said that at the time of Khaled's death he had his own copy saved on his smart phone, as did most of their circle of friends.

Another likely possibility—although one people generally don't like to mention—is that Khaled Saieed had some sort of prior relationship with the local police that had somehow gone sour. Perhaps he was an informant who gave them bad information or was resisting attempts to turn him into an informant. Haitham Mesbah speculates that the officers had no intention of killing Khaled, and that they had orders to simply intimidate the young man or teach him a lesson, but went overboard. But that possibility still leaves open the glaring question of why he was so specifically targeted. It's a mystery that seems unlikely to ever be properly answered, and many of Khaled's friends seem reluctant to delve too deeply into the issue.

"There's still something hidden there," Mesbah acknowledges. "There's only three people who know the truth—the two officers and Khaled."

If the two officers knew the truth, they weren't revealing it to investigators. In July, *Al-Masry Al-Youm* newspaper published a two-part exclusive with inside details of the Khaled Saeed investigation—including transcripts of Mahmoud's and Suleiman's interrogations.

According to the published interrogation transcripts, both officers stuck to the same story—one that contradicts physical evidence and multiple eyewitness accounts. Mahmoud testified that he approached Saieed at the cybercafé because he *was* "wanted in two cases of theft and possession of a knife."

According to Mahmoud, there was never any violence directed against Saieed—not in the café nor in the neighboring stairwell. The young man simply choked to death on the spot without anyone laying a hand on him.

"He was holding something in his hand. When I tried to take it from him, he put it in his mouth and swallowed it," Mahmoud testified. *"Then he fell on the ground and his legs started to shake violently."*

When asked to explain Saieed's injuries, Mahmoud speculated that they all came from the young man's body being mishandled by paramedics. *"All the injuries were caused when he fell off the ambulance's stretcher and as his head hit the ambulance's door. Also the people were hitting him on the face to revive him. He also fell on the floor when he swallowed the wrapped object. But he wasn't bleeding,"* Mahmoud said, according to the transcripts published in *Al-Masry Al-Youm.*

As the case against the two officers moved through the court system, amid continuing protests, the government's strategy deepened and grew meaner. Throughout the fall, the country's newspapers were sprinkled with comments from anonymous security sources claiming Khaled had a long criminal record—including drug dealing and writing bad checks. A September 2010 hearing at the Alexandria criminal courthouse featured a pair of dueling rallies: one group demanding justice for Khaled, and a counterprotest of people expressing support for the police and loudly chanting that Khaled Saieed and his supporters were all drug-addled criminals.

One day, witnesses such as Mohammed Naieem received a visit from a man identifying himself as Mohammed Abdel Aal, head of a political party no one had ever heard of called the Social Justice Party. According to Naieem, Abdel Aal told him, "I'm giving you advice. Don't testify. It won't produce a result."

Slightly rattled after Abdel Aal's visit, Naieem's wife Amal approached Hassan Mesbah, the Space Net café owner for advice. "I told her, 'Follow your conscience. If you don't want to testify, then don't. But don't forget God's balance sheet,'" Mesbah said.

On October 19, the mysterious figure of Mohammed Abdel Aal struck again. Copies of the Social Justice Party's equally obscure newspaper, *The Arab Nation*, appeared in coffee shops throughout the neighborhood containing a nasty multiple-page smear job directed at Khaled, his family, and several of the witnesses. Hassan Mesbah still keeps a copy of the issue in his desk at Space Net. Khaled Saieed is derided in a front-page headline as "The Marijuana Martyr." His mother Leila is (erroneously) quoted in another headline as saying, "My son is a hash-head. So what?" A third headline mocks the fast-growing "We Are All Khaled Saieed" Facebook group by proclaiming, "The group 'We are all hash-heads' demands the harshest possible punishment for the two officers responsible for reducing the number of hash-heads by one."

Inside the newspaper, there was a full-page article by Abdel Aal himself laying out a multitiered accusation that Khaled was a notorious dealer, the Space Net café was the neighborhood drug den, and Naieem, the doorman, was part of this apparently thriving Cleopatra district drug cartel as well. This was some mean-spirited stuff—not terribly imaginative, but mean. Clearly the goal was to restore some of the "He must have deserved it" sentiment among ordinary citizens. The problem was the horrific eyewitness accounts of Khaled's last moments. It's hard to convince people that anyone, no matter what their record, deserves to be publicly beaten to death.

"Even if he was a drug addict, even if he killed thirty people, that's a job for a court and a judge," said Ibrahim, the young veiled mother at the June protest.

Despite the government's efforts, the Khaled Saieed case mushroomed through Egyptian society. Haitham Mesbah credits his friend's death as the real unofficial start of the Egyptian revolution. "After that, people were completely fed up with the police," he said. "There wasn't anybody in Egypt that didn't know who Khaled Saieed was. From that point onward, the whole country started moving."

5

The Rigged Game

My father, who emigrated from Egypt in 1968, likes to tell a pair of stories that shed some insight on the historic state of Egyptian democracy.

The first is from the summer of 1968. President Gamal Abdel Nasser, still reeling from the previous year's thrashing by Israel in the Six-Day War, holds a national referendum that's essentially a yes/no vote of confidence in his wisdom as a leader. A member of my family is in charge of the vote counting in the Nile Delta province of Beheira.

This relative later told my father the vote stuffing was so outrageously over the top that he and other officials spent three days selectively destroying ballots just to get the "yes" votes from 120 percent down to a more seemly 99 percent.

The other is from the autumn of 1987. My late uncle Hamed went to vote in parliamentary elections, and is surprised to find that my father—long since living in

America—is marked down as having voted earlier that day for the government candidate. When my uncle raised this inconvenient fact, the military officer in charge of the polling station sternly told him: "I've known your brother since middle school and I'm telling you, Omar was here and he voted."

Far from creating a scandal or leading to some sort of wider protest, the incident became a running joke in my family. The next time my father visited Egypt, half of his relatives feigned humorous outrage that he would fly from America, vote for the government, and fly back without calling any of them.

The moral of these stories?

First, every Egyptian government in living memory cheated in elections—even when it didn't have to.

Nasser in his time was pretty much the most wildly popular Middle Eastern leader since Salaheddin. In a straight-up contest, he probably would have taken 85 percent of the vote—an overwhelming public mandate by any Western democratic standard. But he still couldn't stomach the uncertainty of a fair vote.

Second, almost every Egyptian absolutely *knew* about the cheating, assumed that it would always be this way, and believed that anybody who tried to resist was a fool.

Egyptians, despite what any statistics say about education or literacy rates, are deeply sophisticated, but also cynical, about politics. Under Mubarak and his predecessors, they knew the score. And for the most part they didn't think they could do anything about it.

———

All of which leads to the absolute fiasco that was the November 28, 2010, parliamentary elections. After months of angrily insisting to the world that it could conduct free and fair elections, Hosni Mubarak's government proceeded to hold one of the most widely decried votes in the nation's modern history.

In terms of pure numbers, the results were a dominating victory for Mubarak's ruling National Democratic Party. NDP candidates captured 473 out of a possible 508 elected seats in the People's Assembly, the lower house of Parliament. There's only one problem with these results: truly nobody who wasn't directly drawing a paycheck from the government believed in them.

Put simply, the numbers produced didn't pass even the most casual smell test—bringing us into the territory of Nasser's old 120 percent approval rating.

The most glaring defect: The Muslim Brotherhood, Egypt's largest and best organized opposition force, went from winning the eighty-eight parliamentary seats they captured in the 2005 elections to exactly one seat.

There's no other way to put it: Mubarak's government simply overplayed its hand. They obviously saw that it was time to put the upstart Brotherhood in its place. But Mubarak's cadres apparently didn't know when to stop, or were simply unable to act with any degree of restraint.

"The regime has over-reached. In opting to wipe out its opposition, and with such lack of subtlety, it has made a major and potentially debilitating miscalculation," wrote Shadi Hamid, research director of the Brookings Doha Center think tank. "The regime has lost whatever legitimacy it had left. More importantly, however, it has breathed new life into what, just one month ago, was an aimless, fractious opposition that couldn't agree on whether or not to boycott the elections."

National Democratic Party officials, in the aftermath of the vote, even seemed to acknowledge this reality—with some admitting that the government may have re-established its dominance but in the process sacrificed both international credibility and any plausible claim that Egypt was on the path to anything resembling a proper democracy.

The state-owned *Al-Ahram* newspaper quoted an anonymous high-level NDP official as saying, "Less would have been more dignifying," for the party and the government's image. "Things did not need to go so far."

The list of electoral violations read like a manual on how to rig a national election. There was intimidation, vote buying, the use of police forces and plainclothes thug squads, denying licensed election observers access to polling places, and of course, good old-fashioned ballot box stuffing.

Local political observers—an understandably cynical bunch by definition—were still shocked at just how far the government went to cook this result.

"At least get creative in how you rig the elections," publisher Hisham Kassem told *The New York Times*. "I was expecting a few more seats for the opposition . . . Nothing can stun me now."

Ibrahim Eissa put the matter in even starker terms. The longtime maverick newspaper editor found himself abruptly unemployed a few weeks before the election in what he claims was a move to limit independent media voices before the vote. In the space of two weeks, Eissa's television talk show was pulled from the air and his firebrand newspaper *Al-Dostour* was purchased by new owners, who promptly fired him.

I met with Eissa in his suburban Cairo home about a week after the elections. A portly, cheerfully cynical professional gadfly, who's almost never seen in public without his trademark glasses and suspenders, Eissa was home in the middle of the day in his pajamas; his preelection blackballing had left him plenty of time to chat. As his young children played upstairs, Eissa described the elections as a turning point on the way to a dark place. It was, he told me, the moment when it finally became clear to everyone that this government (and maybe this society) is simply not capable of reform.

"These last parliamentary elections proved several things. First off, you can't bet on President Mubarak. You can't believe that he's going to change anything. You can't bet on reform from inside the regime. You can't bet on fair elections. You can't bet on the opposition parties. You can't bet on the people themselves, because the people either accepted forgery, or they stayed silent, or they took part in it," Eissa said.

———

Before considering the events of election day itself, a couple of anecdotes are necessary in order to demonstrate the absolutely surreal cognitive dissonance on display in the weeks preceding the vote. On several levels, Mubarak's government was loudly saying one thing while doing the exact opposite—creating an environment where black was white, night was day, and democracy was flourishing in Egypt.

About a week before the elections, I was sitting in a coffee shop around the corner from my home, conducting a telephone interview with George Ishak, a prominent opposition activist and founding member of the Kefaya movement. The topic of the day was the opposition's mounting calls for international monitors of polling places and the government's strident denials that it could handle matters itself without any foreign help or insults to Egypt's sovereignty.

After concluding a rather loud interview about the need for monitors and the pros and cons for an opposition boycott of the elections, I hung up the phone and realized two things: half the coffee shop was looking at me, and most of the customers seemed to be police officers—both uniformed and plainclothes.

Slightly unnerved, I was preparing to pay the check and get the hell out of there when one of the officers (having obviously heard everything I'd been saying) came over and struck up a conversation. He was in civilian clothes with a gun on his hip and his colleagues seemed to be treating him with deference—which made him either a senior police officer or a member of the State Security Investigations. Neither option was good news.

He introduced himself as Major Khaled and started asking my opinion on the upcoming elections. I told him, candidly, that I wasn't optimistic at all; multiple signs pointed to a business-as-usual sham election. There had already been well-documented government crackdowns on Muslim Brotherhood activists ahead of the election, and I knew from my own professional home-base (the English edition of *Al-Masry Al-Youm* newspaper) that local editors were already being pressured by State Security to tone down their coverage. What's more, recent constitutional amendments had removed generally independent Egyptian judges from the polling stations, meaning that everyone was essentially being asked to trust the Egyptian government to run a fair election, with no prior evidence to support that trust.

Major Khaled (I never asked his last name and never told him mine) responded with an elaborate analogy along the lines of, "Imagine if you're a father in charge of a household named Egypt. Would you let a stranger come into your home to make sure you were a good father and protecting the interests of your children?"

I told him that the main problem with Egypt regarding elections is that there was no distinction between the government and the National Democratic Party. Every government function—from police work to election monitoring to the committee that permits the formation of political parties—were all under the control of a single political party. I quoted a prominent Muslim Brotherhood politician who liked to refer to the Interior Ministry as "the military wing of the NDP."

So what chance did any opposition party or candidate have if all the levers of power and enforcement were controlled by a rival party with a vested interest in the results? Egypt would never know true democracy, I told him, until the NDP had just as much power and government control as any other party. As long as the government *was* the NDP, then everything was fake.

The last thing I wanted to do was get into an argument with the State Security officer who was apparently responsible for my neighborhood, so I paid the check and got moving. As I left, Major Khaled told me, "Just have faith. I promise you on election day you will see things you never thought you would see in Egypt."

He seemed so sincere that I almost believed he meant it—that he and his colleague in the security state had received orders to actually play it straight this time.

A few days later, I accompanied a prominent Muslim Brotherhood-affiliated parliamentarian named Moham-med al-Beltagy as he campaigned for re-election in the working-class Cairo district of Shubra al-Kheima. At first, everything seemed fairly normal, almost like a functioning democratic process. Along with a few other journalists, I walked alongside al-Beltagy's sign-carrying supporters, recording their chants and watching the candidate give several brief campaign speeches over a portable loudspeaker.

After about two hours, I got into a taxi along with my friend Ursula Lindsey, a correspondent for the BBC radio program *The World,* and prepared to head home. Suddenly the taxi was stopped by a crowd of plainclothes men, obviously State Security.

They removed us from the taxi, and demanded our IDs and credentials. They aggressively asked us for our *tasreeh* (permission) to work as journalists in this neighborhood. I explained several times that my press card issued by the Ministry of Information *was* my permission. It quickly became very apparent that our official state press cards were worth almost nothing.

What followed was a half hour of surreal tedium—standing on a darkened street with ten plainclothes officers who apparently thought they were protecting the country from us. The officers kept explaining that they were "following orders" but refused to explain just what those orders were.

There were several comments implying that as foreign journalists, we were hopelessly biased against the Egyptian government and only gave attention to opposition groups like the Muslim Brotherhood. At one point, one of them laughed and said, "Welcome to Shubra al-Kheima. Now don't ever come back. Shubra al-Kheima is hazardous to your health."

Finally I was handed a mobile phone. On the other end was a man identifying himself only as "General Ahmed."

He came off as the nicest guy in the world, and told me I was welcome to return to the neighborhood any time I wanted. But there was a catch. "To prevent problems like this in the future," he told me, it would be best if I first stopped by the local police station to inform them of my presence. That way, he said, they could arrange a police escort, "for your protection."

I restrained the urge to point out that the only protection I needed was from his men. Finally we were allowed to leave. But it felt like we had been given a clear window into the methods that a police state uses to control, intimidate, and generally confuse journalists.

The following morning came a surreal postscript. The government held a press conference to discuss their electoral preparations. The head of the state-sponsored National Council for Human Rights issued several assurances that this electoral round would be clean, transparent, and free of the violations that marred previous votes.

Attending the conference, I mentioned that several journalists, including myself, had been detained the previous night simply for doing our jobs. I asked what guarantees the Human Rights Council could provide to ensure that journalists would be able to cover the elections without harassment. The responses were genuinely shocking.

Several government officials—members of the supposedly semi-independent government human rights watchdog council—told me that it was my fault for being there. "If you want to interview a candidate, you should meet them in their office," a council member named Leila

Takla said, literally wagging her finger at me. "But walking alongside a campaign rally, that constitutes political activity."

That last point was my favorite, and an indication of just how detached from any sort of democratic reality Egypt was under the Mubarak regime. Aside from the whole "letting journalists do their job" aspect, there was the implication that I deserved to be harassed by security for appearing to involve myself in "political activity"— which means that any citizen actually participating in such an activity really was fair game in the eyes of the state and deserved whatever treatment they received.

All of which brings us to November 28, 2010: Election Day. I was in Alexandria all day, and visited three polling stations; in two of them I immediately spotted blatant irregularities.

At one polling place in a school in the Suyouf district, things seemed to be progressing normally with a steady trickle of voters approaching the gates. That is until you noticed that almost all the voters were coming from a local youth center one block away.

On the grounds of that youth center I found a virtual mob scene. More than one thousand people were gathered, with more arriving constantly in busses and minivans. I blended into the crowd and walked around. Inside a massive tent structure, multiple clusters of people gathered— each of them thrusting their pink voter cards at different men holding highlighter pens. The men would, in turn, make a mark on each card and hand it back.

Utterly mystified, I quietly approached a middle-aged man, flashed my press card, told him I didn't care about his name, and asked just what was going on.

"These are all civil servants like me," he told me. "They're selling their votes for fifty Egyptian pounds [about nine dollars]."

When I asked the significance of the highlighter mark, he said, "The mark means they will let you in easily at the door of the polling station. If you don't have that mark, they'll run you around and make it hard for you to enter."

As I was leaving, he gave me a classically Egyptian cynical take on the state of local democracy. His conclusion: the government here had become very adept at producing the surface sheen of a democratic process—complete with banners, rallies, and glass-walled ballot boxes. But the reality on the ground was a completely different issue.

"If you listen to the things the government is saying about transparency [a word he pronounced with heavy sarcasm] and free elections, it sounds very convincing," he said. "Until you see it in the streets, they sound like they mean it."

At a second Alexandria polling station, I found a man named Mohammed Fawzi standing across the street from the entrance, with a nice, shiny, new election monitor badge from the government's Higher Electoral Commission hanging around his neck.

In theory, these badges gave him the right to enter any polling station and observe the actual vote taking place—all part of the government's "we can handle our own monitoring" policy.

"It has no value," Fawzi told me. "They banned us from entering."

When I asked why the police officer at the polling station gate had shrugged off his ID, Fawzi just smiled and said, "It's Egypt."

So instead of observing the ballot box, Fawzi was reduced to nervously standing across the street and staying one step ahead of the uniformed and plainclothes police presence.

"They've militarized the whole neighborhood," he said.

When I pulled out my cell phone to take a picture, Fawzi quickly stopped me—saying that police were grabbing anybody with a camera. Within a minute of Fawzi's warning, that's exactly what happened to a young man standing two feet away from me. Police took his camera and hustled him inside the polling place gates. Fawzi approached and took a peek and told me he saw the young photographer being aggressively strip-searched. To avoid that fate, Fawzi told me he was taking pictures by pretending to talk on his cell phone and using the built-in camera to sneak in the occasional shot.

Keep in mind that this was an official election monitor licensed by the Egyptian government forced to engage in guerrilla tactics just to photograph the *outside* of the polling station where he was supposed to be inside monitoring. That more than anything encapsulates what happened on election day. No matter what rosy promises were made leading up to the vote, no matter how many times government officials promised fairness and transparency, at the end of the day every polling place was the absolute, unquestioned property of the police state—which made it the property of the NDP.

Fawzi was clearly a little uneasy about talking to me in front of the police, so I took him around the corner to a coffee shop where we could speak freely. A third-year engineering student at Alexandria University, he was depressed and visibly upset by the day's events. The poor guy obviously came into the elections thinking he would be taking part in Egypt's path on the road to democracy.

"Things aren't going well at all," he said between nervous drags on a cigarette. "I expected it would be a little cleaner than this. Here it's like they're telling you who will be your representative."

There was nothing truly egregious taking place, he said; nobody at his station got their head bashed in trying to cast their vote or anything. It was just the tedious banality of a rigged game—the ever-present busloads of paid-off civil servants, the plainclothes government goons circulating through the crowd, and above everything else, the determination to minimize the number of independent eyes on the ballot boxes inside.

Polling places around the country reported these sorts of incidents and worse. There were multiple cases of violence, usually riot cops clashing with enraged voters who believed their district was being tampered with.

"The whole thing is incredibly fraudulent. There's no

way to escape that," said Samer Shehata, a Georgetown University professor specializing in Arab politics and a native Alexandrian. "It's so structurally rigged in so many different ways that the regime doesn't need to hit people on the head to get the outcome they want."

It was, for many Egyptians, final, definitive proof that this government was, in fact, regressing and was incapable of ever reforming itself. But there was also a distinct whiff of desperation about the whole deal. The government's actions seemed rash, clumsy, and a little panicked. It simply wasn't the sort of thing a confident dictatorship does.

The government's parliamentary overkill only deepened the pervasive sense in Egypt that things were approaching some sort of endgame. One of the interpretations of the government's take-no-prisoners approach to these elections is that it was stacking the deck in preparation for something big the following year. But if so, just what were they preparing for?

Some sort of father-to-son inheritance scenario was the most frequently mentioned possibility. But there was also growing sentiment that all this leash-tightening was just leading to things remaining exactly the way they are.

"Maybe it's preparation to keep the situation the same. It's about ending any hope by Egyptians for political change," said Eissa, the blackballed newspaper editor. "If you ask me, I'm not expecting inheritance. President Mubarak will continue in power, and he doesn't need to leave power—even for his son."

Still, the parliamentary fiasco didn't anger or galvanize people the way that Khaled Saieed's death five months earlier did. The activist ranks remained steadfast, to a certain extent, probably enjoying the sight of the regime opening itself up to international embarrassment. But among the average apolitical citizens, it was dispiriting and frightening. Far from a call to arms, it was taken as a clear sign that something much worse was coming.

In fact, something big *was* coming, but it wasn't what the people, and certainly not the regime, expected.

6

The ElBaradei Effect

Mohammed ElBaradei returned to his native land to a reception worthy of a rock star. More than one thousand cheering supporters flooded into the Cairo International Airport in February 2010 to greet the man who had suddenly been vaulted into the position of Egypt's savior. The crush of well-wishers was so dense that ElBaradei had to leave the airport terminal though a side exit.

One of the people at the airport that day was Maha Elgamal, the mid-forties upper-class homemaker who would spend much of 2010 passionately volunteering for ElBaradei's cause.

"I really respect him. He's sincere, honest, and straightforward," Elgamal said. "ElBaradei didn't invent the wheel of change in Egypt. But he really got things moving here."

Just a few months before, ElBaradei had stepped down as head of the International Atomic Energy Agency and immediately launched a series of scathing interviews decrying Mubarak's Egypt. From the very beginning, it was clear that ElBaradei had tapped into something primal in the beleaguered Egyptian political psyche. People seemed to look to him as their salvation, the hero on a white horse who would single-handedly save the country from a Gamal Mubarak succession scenario. ElBaradei had managed to become a rallying point for the vast ABG (Anybody-But-Gamal) voter bloc.

Even before his return to Egypt, ElBaradei had begun to inspire unprecedented acts of creative subversion among Egyptians, akin to a spontaneous viral marketing campaign. Young people were detained for spray painting pro-ElBaradei slogans on buildings and bridges; one inspired restaurant owner (quoted anonymously in Ibrahim Eissa's feisty independent paper *Al-Dostour*) had begun stamping the cash he took in with pro-ElBaradei slogans, then re-circulating the money.

The independent media became obsessed with him, while the state-owned newspapers made a brief and disastrous attempt at a smear campaign—painting the longtime Vienna resident as a meddling expatriate who hadn't lived in Egypt for decades, and just might have a foreign passport and suspect loyalties.

A December 2009 column by Osama Saraya, editor of the state-owned flagship daily *Al-Ahram*, called ElBaradei "ill-informed," and labeled his entire one-man reform campaign, "tantamount to a constitutional coup."

The effort backfired, drawing the heavy criticism of the state media. After that, they mostly pursued a policy of pretending that the Nobel laureate didn't exist—an approach that often led to hilarious results. On the day after ElBaradei's arrival, when his picture dominated the front page of every independent and opposition newspaper, *Al-Ahram* ran a nine-line brief, below the front-page fold, frostily noting that a Foreign Ministry representative had gone to the airport to welcome ElBaradei.

ElBaradei hit the ground running, and for several months he seemed absolutely bulletproof. In his first week back in the country, he appeared on a popular talk show hosted by Mona al-Shazli. The interview left ElBaradei's popularity soaring and al-Shazli fending off accusations of being a regime apologist.

In calm measured tones, ElBaradei, a lawyer and diplomat by training, basically destroyed his host. When al-Shazli told him that most Egyptian citizens "benefit from the stability" provided by the Mubarak regime, ElBaradei responded, "Let's not fool ourselves. If a person can't find food, can't find medical treatment, and can't find education, there's no stability."

For a couple months, ElBaradei-mania ran wild. He appeared on multiple talk shows and the independent press breathlessly covered his movements, meetings, and the formation of his National Association for Change. Amazingly, the state-owned newspapers and television stations continued to act like he didn't exist.

ElBaradei announced a campaign to gather millions of signatures supporting a list of demands that included repealing the country's "emergency laws" and eliminating obstacles to an independent presidential candidacy.

His young volunteers—many of them drawn from the sidelines and into politics by ElBaradei himself—fanned out in a nationwide petition drive.

In the summer of 2010, I accompanied a group of ElBaradei volunteers gathering signatures in Hadayek Helwan, a middle-class Cairo suburb, permanently coated in dust from nearby quarries and cement factories. The evening was a clear window not only into the power of ElBaradei's appeal but also to the twin obstacles of complacency and fear that he faced.

The volunteers, led by volunteer Maha Elgamal, were a diverse bunch—Muslims and Christians, veiled women alongside fashionable ladies in tight jeans with bejeweled belt buckles. They worked their way up the street, approaching passersby, local fruit sellers, and storeowners, even calling up to residents looking down from their balconies.

ElBaradei's seven-point list of petition demands amounted to sweeping domestic reform and would have required the rewriting of three separate articles of the constitution. It included the establishment of international polling place monitoring and the removal of legal obstacles designed to prevent an independent presidential candidacy.

But it was the first demand—the immediate repeal of the emergency laws—that struck the strongest chord with ordinary citizens, and ElBaradei's volunteers knew that was their strongest card to play.

"We're with the National Association for Change, Dr. ElBaradei's organization. We want to cancel the emergency laws," Elgamal told one resident, trying to secure another signature.

Abdulla Sultan, a twenty-year-old college student, had never even heard of ElBaradei before but agreed to sign the petition as soon as he heard the emergency law demand.

"That's all I need to hear," he said.

Across the street, Hala al-Banay signed up Mohammed Fathi, a thirty-two-year-old civil servant who moonlights at a neighborhood photo studio.

"The first request is to lift the emergency law under which so many people have been arrested," she said.

"A lot of people," Fathi responded.

"That's right. People you know and I know."

"I just hope this works. I'm tired of the way things are. Hopefully this is the beginning of the end."

After securing Fathi's signature and national ID number on the petition, al-Banay said, "You know this isn't the end for you. Spread the word and get involved in any kind of political activity. Start your own group if you want."

Their style was persistent, positive, and occasionally confrontational. For instance Mahitab Jellani, a young veiled woman and longtime political activist, kept a copy in her purse of Khaled Saieed's iconic autopsy photo, pulling it out to remind the undecided about the casual daily police brutality that had become commonplace under the emergency laws. But not every reaction was positive. One storeowner refused to sign, saying, "I don't really care about politics. I mind my own business and nobody bothers me."

Safaa Saieed, a volunteer wearing a pink scarf over her hair, told another young veiled woman, "We're not asking you to vote for anyone in particular. This is about more voting rights for all of us."

The young woman seemed intensely interested, but a teenage man accompanying her kept interrupting Saieed's pitch, trying to drag his companion away by the arm, saying, "Let's go. They're going to get us in trouble."

Finally Saieed snapped at him, "We're trying to create an honorable country. People like you are what's dragging us backwards."

The woman left without signing, but took a petition and asked about ways to sign online; Saieed was annoyed nonetheless.

"If he wasn't here, she would have signed on the spot," she said.

Despite the obstacles, that spring and summer of 2010 was an exciting time for ElBaradei's campaign. His people seemed inspired and his message was gaining momentum.

"I think I was a rallying force for all this anger building up," ElBaradei told me in an interview several months later. "I had a sort of immunity so I could speak a little louder."

Then it all went wrong. His organization foundered, largely through his own decisions and failings. He refused to join in with street protests, disappointing many of the hard-core activists who wanted him to lead from the front. His travel schedule kept him outside of Egypt so much that it became a running joke among his senior deputies. His own campaign spokesman wrote an angry editorial criticizing ElBaradei for not spending more time at home.

The reasons for ElBaradei's loss of momentum were multiple. For starters, despite people's expectations of him, the bookish former diplomat proved himself anything but an instinctive politician. He rarely appeared in public, and when he did, ElBaradei seemed distinctly uncomfortable with the masses.

Even longtime supporters like Maha Elgamal found themselves disillusioned by the internal dynamics of the ElBaradei campaign. "It was a disaster," she said, adding that ElBaradei surrounded himself with amateurs and opportunists who were never on the same page with each other. "As Egyptians, one of our problems is that we don't know how to work together."

Hassan Nafaa served as one of ElBaradei's senior deputies and advisors. The longtime Cairo University political science professor had always been a trusted source for independent-minded political analysis and had emerged in the early years of the twenty-first century as a vocal critic of the Mubarak regime, writing and speaking out forcefully against the Gamal Mubarak Project. When ElBaradei launched his reform campaign, the two men joined forces and Nafaa became General Coordinator of the National Association for Change. The union made perfect sense; Nafaa could provide the local knowledge and experience with the Egyptian political scene that ElBaradei understandably lacked.

But Nafaa eventually parted ways with the campaign and now speaks bitterly of the experience. "I think El-Baradei wasted a very big opportunity, a historic opportunity," he said.

The primary point of contention, Nafaa recalls, was ElBaradei's insistence on maintaining an almost comically busy travel schedule and his reluctance to take to the streets. "We told him he was needed here in the playing field," Nafaa said. "Had he decided to stay here more and to interact more with the real people in the streets and to go and attend conferences and so on, he could have become the real symbol of the changes that happened in Egypt."

This refusal to heed the desperate pleas of even his senior advisors represented a larger personal failing, according to Nafaa. He described ElBaradei as imperious, stubborn, and more used to issuing orders than considering contrary opinions.

By the time he resigned from the NAC in late 2010, "I was absolutely sure that this was not the right man to lead an opposition movement," Nafaa said.

A pivotal moment in understanding ElBaradei came on June 25, 2010, when he attended—amid great hype—the protest in Alexandria in memory of Khaled Saieed. Anger was running high, especially in Alexandria, and ordinary apolitical citizens were starting to uncharacteristically take to the streets. ElBaradei's planned attendance had stoked expectations that this would be the real start of his street-level campaign against the Mubarak regime.

Instead he lasted less than ten minutes in public, waving to the crowd and giving a short interview to CNN before departing. The disappointment among spectators was palpable. In contrast, Hamdeen Sabahi, a veteran opposition activist and independent parliamentarian, was still there an hour later in a sweat-soaked suit, hugging well-wishers, posing for pictures, and generally acting like a real politician.

Six months later, I interviewed ElBaradei for more than an hour at his home in a posh gated community near the Pyramids. He struck me as a sincere, intelligent man who clearly understood the depths of Egypt's problems and was upset about all the right things. He was also a bit arrogant, stubborn, and extremely sheltered; I couldn't help but ask him about that day in Alexandria.

When I put forth the theory that he just didn't seem comfortable being the center of attention in large crowds, the normally self-assured and verbose ElBaradei actually stammered a bit, seemingly lost for words. His wife Aida, who was sitting with us, chimed in reassuringly, "Don't worry, you'll get better at it."

In recalling that demonstration, ElBaradei made a comment that speaks volumes about his life experience. He remembered emerging from the downtown Alexandria mosque after noon prayers and surveying the three-thousand-strong crowd, surrounded as usual by a massive deployment of black-clad riot police.

"It was the first time I've seen all this Central Security. It was like a war zone. It was an amazing scene to me to realize how repressive and how much of a police state we have become," he told me.

I was shocked; the fact that he had never seen a Central Security deployment basically meant that he had never attended a single demonstration in Egypt. I must have witnessed the Central Security tactics at work at least fifty times, getting teargassed more often than I can remember—and I wasn't even a protester. For someone launching a high-profile confrontation with the Egyptian government, he had literally no street-level experience into how a police state actually worked and kept power.

As the parliamentary elections approached in November 2010, ElBaradei's campaign seemed to steadily lose steam. The real death knell came when the Muslim Brotherhood—which had partnered up with his petition campaign and used its considerable grassroots machine to help gather signatures—chose to defy his call for a blanket opposition boycott of the elections. Without the Brotherhood on board, any boycott would be meaningless. By election day, ElBaradei had somehow gone from being Egypt's political savior to a borderline nonentity.

In retrospect, the Brotherhood's decision to break with ElBaradei and contest the parliamentary elections probably sped the path toward revolution. The sight of the organization instantly going from eighty-eight Parliament seats to zero was so ridiculous that it immediately discredited the elections and the legitimacy of the new Parliament.

But the Brotherhood's leaders couldn't have known at the time that the NDP would bungle the elections so badly. If the government had displayed the slightest degree of subtlety in its election rigging, the Brotherhood's stance would be remembered far less fondly. Essentially, by abandoning ElBaradei and entering the elections, the Brotherhood played right into the government's hands—only to watch the government hand the moral victory right back to them.

"It wasn't the Brotherhood that did it. It was the stupidity of the government," said Elgamal, the ElBaradei volunteer. "The Brotherhood was wrong to enter the elections. If the government had been smart enough to give them thirty seats, it would have come out with more legitimacy."

By early 2011, ElBaradei and his movement had essentially been marginalized. His critics saw it as entirely fitting that he was in Vienna on January 25, 2011, when it all started. He was regarded as a television studio politician, comfortable giving interviews and lectures but with no taste for street politics and no affinity for the people.

Part of that is certainly true, but it doesn't give ElBaradei enough credit—both for the prerevolutionary role he played and for the good he may continue to do in the future.

One of the reasons people were so disappointed in him, was that they had an unrealistic expectation of what he actually was. To his credit, ElBaradei has always been up-front in declaring that he had no desire to be Egypt's savior.

"I keep saying, 'I am not the messiah.' I keep, if you like, dampening their expectations. If you are waiting for a horseman on a white horse, the bad news is he's not coming," ElBaradei said in December 2010. "I don't want to replace a one-person regime with another one-person regime. I'm trying to convert Egypt into institutions."

The problem was that most people simply refused to take him at face value, expecting ElBaradei to play a role that he was both unwilling and ill suited to play. He was overrated for so long that he eventually became under-rated. In the process, many have lost sight of the significant positive contributions he made, and the strong possibility that he personally helped speed the end of the Mubarak era.

ElBaradei certainly didn't invent the resistance, but he helped serve as one of its focal points and helped mainstream many of the issues that had been bubbling for years. He skillfully used his international name and notoriety to pressure and embarrass the Mubarak regime on the global stage.

Even Nafaa, who has very few kind words to say about his former colleague, acknowledges the significance of

ElBaradei's contribution to Egypt's prerevolutionary environment.

"For someone of his stature to say, 'I'm against the oppression of the state' was a very big thing," Nafaa said. "People were saying, 'If not Gamal, then who?' And ElBaradei provided that plausible alternative. It was important to show that there were other personalities beyond Gamal and Hosni Mubarak."

ElBaradei also helped popularize the notion that change in Egypt needed to come from outside the country's existing "opposition" parties—which he summarily dismissed as co-opted and toothless extensions of the regime. Again these weren't new ideas in the Egyptian political arena, but ElBaradei used his name recognition to help these ideas reach new ears.

One of the more revealing aspects of ElBaradei's return was watching these official opposition parties struggle to find an honorable stance to take on him. He was, after all, writing off existing parties like the Wafd as part of a pseudo-democratic façade. Mounir Fakhry Abdel Nour, Secretary General of the Wafd Party (and later the Minister of Tourism in the first post-Mubarak government), made sure to praise ElBaradei as "a breath of fresh air that inspired a lot of youth and rocked the boat." But he also said that if ElBaradei wanted to become a "legitimate force for change," he needed to join an existing party.

"The natural, safe, and respectable organization or machine is a political party—a party as opposed to a protest movement. A party has a life span; it's a responsible organization because you can monitor their positions. You can't do that with a protest movement because it's an ad hoc movement and you can't really follow," Abdel Nour told me. "But when you're talking about the 6th of April movement, who is the 6th of April? When you're talking about Kefaya, who is Kefaya?"

Abdel Nour's stance was a clear example of exactly the kind of calcified thinking that ElBaradei was publicly rejecting. It's completely ridiculous that Abdel Nour in 2010 would take the April 6 and Kefaya movement—two of the most influential phenomena of the past decade— and dismiss them out of hand simply because they weren't a member of his club. It was exactly this kind of thinking that was the reason people were so hungry for an outside-the-system alternative. If ElBaradei's arrival helped drive the final nail in the coffin of Egypt's fake opposition, then he deserved to be lauded for that alone, regardless of his failings.

During the revolution, ElBaradei received his first-ever whiff of tear gas on January 28. He only made one appearance in Tahrir Square during the two weeks it was held by protesters. But his appearance caused such a chaotic mob scene that he can be forgiven for not returning. He was, for all intents and purposes, irrelevant to the process. ElBaradei meant more outside of Egypt than inside. But that doesn't mean he didn't help lay some of the groundwork for the revolution.

With Mubarak out of the picture and no regime to oppose, ElBaradei's true popularity and appeal is an open question, but he still remains a political force. The surest proof of that is that ElBaradei is still worth plotting against.

During a March 19 nationwide referendum on a package of constitutional amendments, ElBaradei was attacked by an angry mob while attempting to vote in the lower-class Cairo district of Moqattum. Journalists and witnesses on the scene confirmed that the mob was basically waiting in ambush for ElBaradei, who had (perhaps unwisely) announced days in advance where he would cast his vote. Exactly who organized the ambush remains a mystery, and the authorities don't seem motivated to find out.

ElBaradei's name has become a bit of a joke in many circles, which is an unfair response to his contribution. Even if he doesn't become president of Egypt, ElBaradei would make a fine Foreign Minister or Minister of Justice—provided his ego would allow him to serve, Hillary Clinton–style, in someone else's cabinet.

Either way, Mohammed ElBaradei deserves to be regarded and remembered for his prerevolutionary role and his willingness to publicly confront Mubarak's government. He certainly didn't do it alone, but many of the contributions he made couldn't have come from anyone else. Whatever his failings, ElBaradei helped set the stage for the Egyptian revolution.

7

Uncharted Waters

The events of January 25, 2011, may have come as a shock, even to those who participated. But it was no overnight phenomenon—more like the suddenly flowering of seeds patiently planted over the preceding decade-plus.

"I was shocked. Everyone was. I don't believe anyone who says they knew it would be like that. I had an ear-to-ear smile on the whole day," said Wael Khalil, who had been working for revolution among socialist activists for the past twenty years. "I think of it like concentric circles. It started with a small circle of activists. Kefaya expanded the circle, the 2005 elections expanded the circle. Khaled Saieed was huge."

Nobody was quite sure just what to expect that day. A group of young activists, depending heavily on social media, had announced a day of mass protests, partially in honor of the successful Tunisian revolution eleven days earlier. January 25, a Tuesday, was mischievously chosen because it was also a national holiday: Police Day. The holiday commemorates the 1952 struggle of the Ismailia police force against the occupying British. In the minds of the activists it became a focal point for an outraged condemnation of the behavior of police and the Interior Ministry in general. The idea of subverting Police Day had actually started the year before when the April 6 Movement had held a small protest on January 25, 2010, when the day was first established as a national holiday; that protest was violently broken up and dozens were arrested.

Mohamed Adel, an April 6 spokesman, told a local newspaper, "Egypt's police have become [criminals] who don't care about protecting the people, unlike the heroes of 1952."

There was, among some quarters, a certain satisfaction in turning Police Day on its head. As Nora Shalaby, an archeologist and passionate social media activist put it in a tweet around noon on the twenty-fifth:

It's really satisfying to c Egyptian police officers working & anxious on their day off #jan25

It wasn't the first, or even the tenth, day of mass national protests called for in the previous few years. But this one did feel a little different going in. The wounds of Khaled Saieed and the mass insult of the parliamentary elections were still fresh in the public psyche. A growing number of citizens were simply ceasing to care about the potential consequences of political action. A politically desensitized population was being re-politicized by their unacceptable realities. The old Egyptian saying of "Walk next to the wall"—mind your business, feed your family, and don't get involved in matters of governance above your station—was becoming irrelevant; simply minding your own business in Egypt in 2011 still wouldn't protect you from economic insecurity, institutionalized corruption, nepotistic hiring practices, or a predatory police state.

Most important there was Tunisia, where Mohammed Bouazizi's public suicide in mid-December had touched off a solid month of growing street protests. By January 14, this unprecedented uprising had driven president-for-life Zine al-Abideen Ben Ali into exile. It's impossible to overstate the impact of the Tunisian model. Simply seeing that it could be done—that a sustained public and peaceful mass movement could force out an entrenched dictator—changed everyone's perceptions instantly. After that, all bets were off. There was an immediate post-Tunisia adrenaline rush in the Egyptian activist community—not to mention the uncounted ranks of the depoliticized, who suddenly allowed themselves to think the unthinkable.

Bottom line: without Tunisia, there *is* no Egyptian revolution.

Columnist Ahmed el-Sawi, writing in *Al-Masry Al-Youm* newspaper on January 16, lyrically captured the post-Tunisia mood of new possibilities.

People can nurse grievances for a long time and politicians are incapable of predicting when the masses will express their frustrations. People can be patient, tricking dictators into believing that they have given up. But when they revolt, their anger threatens to unseat leaders and bring down regimes. The events in Tunisia have caused people across the region to feel the winds of change. Tunisia was not plagued with sectarian problems or threatened with partition; it just suffered from immense levels of state repression and corruption, much like other Arab countries. Who will be the first to learn the lessons from Tunisia, the rulers or the ruled?

As the Tunisian poet Abul Qasem Al-Shabi once wrote, "If a people decide to live, destiny must obey."

Maybe something would have happened here at some point, without Tunisia. Public dissatisfaction was peaking, but it had peaked before. In early January, it still seemed very likely that Mubarak and his regime would at least last out the remaining years of his life. The only real question was whether he would chose to unleash whatever succession scenario most believed was waiting in the wings while he was still in office, or whether the entire plot would spring to life after his death. Even those who didn't believe that Gamal Mubarak was destined to succeed his father pinned their objections on something other than a public rejection of his ascension. Hisham Kassem, the independent publisher and former parliamentary candidate, said the military would ultimately object to taking orders from a civilian; Ibrahim

Eissa, the former *Al-Dostour* editor, told me he didn't believe Hosni Mubarak was willing to transfer power to his
son or anyone else. Nobody was willing to predict that the
Egyptian people would reject Gamal or any other succession scenario. Of course the people would eventually accept it. They always had before.

But despite the long-practiced Egyptian tendency toward cynicism and defeatism, there was Tunisia. It was
huge and impossible to deny, and it was spreading. On
January 17 came the first Bouazizi-inspired public cry of
desperation from the heart of the Egyptian capital. A
restaurant owner named Abdou Abdel Hamid from the
Suez Canal city of Qantara set himself on fire in front of
the Parliament Building, about two blocks from Tahrir
Square. Security guards and passing motorists quickly
doused the flames and Abdel Hamid survived his injuries, but the mere fact of his attempt set the country on
edge. Like Bouazizi, Abdel Hamid's grievance was pinned
on a banal governmental dispute; news reports indi-
cated that he had been squabbling with local authorities
over his allotment of monthly coupons for subsidized
bread.

For a while self-immolations in the Arab World became a sort of grisly fad, popping up in Algeria, Mauritania, and several more times in Egypt.

Tunisia and its widening aftereffects essentially hijacked a top-level Arab League economic summit that I
attended in mid-January in the Red Sea town of Sharm

El Sheikh. It was ostensibly a chance for Arab economic ministers and business magnates to gather and discuss the financial future of the region. But from the very start, the still-fresh Tunisian revolution was the elephant in the room—one which grew louder and harder to ignore seemingly with each passing hour. The summit delegates and various ministers didn't go out of their way to mention Tunisia, but they could hardly help talking about it since every journalist they met made a point of asking.

News of Abdel Hamid's suicide attempt in front of the Egyptian parliament broke less than an hour before Arab League Secretary General Amr Moussa and Egypt's trade minister Rachid Mohamed Rachid were scheduled to hold a joint press conference. News of the parallel self-immolation attempt in Mauritania came through on everybody's smart phones during that same press conference.

At one point, I managed to get two minutes with Moussa, and immediately asked him what the lessons were from the Tunisian example. His response (a week before January 25) was surprisingly direct for a career Arab diplomat. "It's an obvious lesson," he said. "The people will no longer accept to be marginalized and pressurized like this."

Throughout the three-day summit, Moussa was memorably off-message. While almost everyone else was understandably downplaying the possibility of a regional Tunisia effect, Moussa was openly warning about the possibility. Moussa's status as a potential reformist post-Mubarak president is certainly questionable given

that he excelled and prospered under the Mubarak regime; but he deserves credit for having had fantastic political instincts. In a speech at the Arab League summit,
Moussa stated that "the Arab soul has been crushed and
broken" by poverty, economic desperation, and political
marginalization.

Rachid, the Egyptian trade minister, flatly stated that
he didn't believe Egypt was in danger of the same sort of
widespread civil unrest as Tunisia. A successful executive at Unilever before being brought into the government, Rachid perhaps can't be blamed for viewing the
issue through a purely economic lens. The reason Egypt
would be safe from a Tunisia-style revolution, he argued,
is that Egypt offered a more comprehensive public subsi-
dies package that ensured affordable fuel and basic food
staples.

"Egypt is a different case than Tunisia. It's not likely
that a crisis like what's happening in Tunisia will happen in Egypt," he said. "Tunisia like many other Arab
countries stopped subsidizing food and petroleum items
many years ago . . . It became very volatile to any changes
in world prices, that's why consumers were directly hit
and consequently frustration escalated."

But despite Rachid's rather narrow interpretation, the
parallels between Tunisia and Egypt were myriad and
impossible to deny. Both featured aging autocrats running what Egyptian economist Ragui Assad likes to call
"kleptocracies"—rule by the thieves. Both were military
regimes that were gradually slipping into monarchies as
a single family and their hangers-on involved themselves

in most aspects of public and economic life. Most important, both had developed into ruling systems that displayed a casual indifference to the needs and desires of their citizens that bordered on open contempt.

All through the Sharm economic summit, there remained a rock-solid insistence by basically everyone but Moussa that what happened in Tunisia would not and could not spread beyond that tiny nation's borders. One journalist, who requested anonymity, recalls discussing the phenomenon with Hossam Zaki–Moussa's right-hand man and currently a senior Foreign Ministry official. Zaki at first dismissed any connection between Tunisia and Egypt. When the journalist pointed out that three Egyptians had set themselves on fire that day, Zaki seemed momentarily taken aback. Then he shrugged and said, "Well those are three from eighty million."

In the midst of the summit came one final embarrassment for the regime, one that personally exposed Hosni Mubarak to direct ridicule. Wael Khalil, the socialist activist, posted on his blog evidence that a widely published picture showing Mubarak in the White House during recent Israeli-Palestinian peace negotiations had been blatantly altered to enhance Mubarak's position. The original Reuters photograph showed Mubarak walking in a phalanx with Israeli Prime Minister Benjamin Netanyahu and Palestinian Authority chief Mahmoud Abbas, all of them arrayed a few steps behind Barack

Obama. The version that ran in *Al-Ahram* looked exactly the same, except somehow Mubarak was now a step ahead of Obama as if he was leading the whole procession through the White House with Obama deferring to him.

Khalil, a thin friendly man with a salt-and-pepper beard, literally beams at the memory of how fast the photo scandal went global, prompting an embarrassing batch of news articles openly mocking Mubarak.

"Their own arrogance and audacity brought them down," he said with a grin. "Suddenly everything was turning against the regime. It was only a matter of a date and time."

All of which led to January 25. Up until that morning, organizers really could only guess what kind of turnout there would be.

"I have to admit, a few days before I wasn't taking it seriously," said Mahmoud Salem. He and his friends would swap jokes about "where the after-revolution party would be."

A Facebook page announcing the protests had commitments to attend from eighty thousand people. But clicking your mouse on "yes" on a Facebook page was a lot different from actually leaving your home and braving the tear gas and truncheons of Central Security; and frankly, prior local history had only enforced the belief that Egyptians—no matter what their level of frustration— would never truly rise up against anything short of a foreign occupation.

"The whole day [on January 24] everyone was contemplating whether to go or not and asking each other whether they were going," said Mohab Wahby, a young development specialist and graduate of the American University in Cairo.

The only reason anyone had any reason to expect that things would be different was because of Tunisia. But for that reason alone, anticipation was running high and battle lines were being drawn. The days preceding January 25 witnessed a succession of preliminary maneuvers on both sides. Local media speculated about whether shopkeepers would forgo the normal holiday shopping sprees and close down for fear of violence. A multitude of Egyptian political factions and movements announced their support and intention to participate.

Khalil and his compatriots were extremely active in those last pre-revolution days. A mysterious PDF file circulated widely in this final week. Written anonymously and entitled "Revolution 2011," the twenty-six-page document amounted to a DIY how-to guide for overthrowing the Egyptian police state. It included detailed city maps advising protesters where to gather, tips on what to wear, recommended chants to draw out undecided citizens, and tactical advice on how to attack police lines, how to limit and treat tear-gas exposure, and how to use spray paint to obscure the windows of the Central Security vans.

One week before the protest, on January 18, an unlikely protagonist suddenly took over the national stage. Asmaa Mahfouz, a twenty-six-year-old veiled woman who was active in the April 6 movement, posted a four-minute YouTube video that went instantly viral.

Speaking directly to the camera, and using plain language that avoided political doublespeak, Mahfouz persuasively cast the upcoming protests as a simple call for national honor and dignity. She never said the word "democracy" and never mentioned the emergency laws, the elections, or Gamal Mubarak. It was all about honor and dignity—words she emphasized again and again in a nearly hypnotic rhythm.

"Four Egyptians have set themselves on fire thinking maybe we can have a revolution like Tunisia. Maybe we can have freedom, justice, honor, and human dignity, not live like animals," she said. "We want to go down to Tahrir Square on January 25th. If we want to have honor and want to live in dignity then we have to go down on January 25th."

Mahfouz's video is one of the underreported aspects of that crucial, brief interregnum between the Tunisian and Egyptian revolutions. Speaking in a rush without notes or pauses, seemingly without stopping to breathe, she issues a direct challenge to a nation of defeatist fence-sitters, making it clear that anyone who didn't participate on January 25 had earned her personal contempt and had only themselves to blame for the circumstances of their lives. A Cairo University graduate with a degree in business administration, Mahfouz directs more of her anger at her fellow Egyptian civilians than at the government and police, almost mercilessly taunting viewers to prove their manhood to her.

"If you think of yourself as a man, come out. Whoever says that women shouldn't go to protests because they'll get beaten, let him have some honor and manhood and come out in the streets on January 25 . . . Anyone who says, 'The numbers will be small and nothing will happen,' I want to say that you are the traitor—just like the president, just like any corrupt official, just like the security officer who beats us . . . Speak to your neighbors, your colleagues at work, your family and friends and encourage them to come. You don't have to come to Tahrir. Just go out in the streets anywhere and take a stand saying you are free human beings. Sitting at home following us on the news and on Facebook only leads to our humiliation. It leads to *my* humiliation. If you have honor and dignity as a man, then come out. Come out and protect me and the other girls at the protest. If you stay at home, you deserve everything that happens to you. And you will be guilty before your nation and before your people. You'll be responsible for everything that happens to us on the street while you sit at home."

In a brilliant conclusion, she actually quotes the Quran, section 13, saying God *"will not change the condition of a people until they change what is in themselves."*

It's impossible to measure just how much of an impact Mahfouz's video manifesto truly had. But anecdotally, several people in the first week of the revolution cited her by name as one of the reasons they turned out for protests. It remains a remarkable moment of viral political marketing, one that cut directly to the heart of the modern Egyptian psyche. Egyptian women took inspiration from her example, and men saw Mahfouz as direct challenge to their prized self-perceptions of what it meant to be a man. Here was a tiny veiled girl who was fearless and angry, literally daring multiple generations of Egyptian men to prove that they have as much courage, dignity, and (metaphorical) balls as she does. Silence, complacency, apathy, and fear—these were all lumped together by Mahfouz as aspects of the same betrayal, the same proof of a fundamental lack of honor.

Late in the evening on January 24, Mahfouz posted a second video. This one was markedly different in tone. She was conciliatory and encouraging, seemingly seeking to assuage people's last-minute fears.

"All of Egypt waits for tomorrow. I know we are all nervous and anxious, but we all want to see tomorrow's event happen and succeed," she said. "I'd like to tell everyone that tomorrow is not the revolution and is not the day that we will change it all. No, tomorrow is the beginning of the end. Tomorrow we make our stand despite all that the security will do to us and stand as one in a peaceful protest. It will be the first real step on the road to change."

The angry tough-love Mahfouz of the first video had been transformed. She appeared encouraged by all the grassroots political work she had witnessed in the preceding week, talking about seeing everyone from young children to elderly pensioners distributing fliers and spreading the word about the protests.

"The most beautiful thing about it is that those who

worked on this were not politicians at all. It was all of us. All Egyptians, we worked hard. Children no older than fourteen! They printed the posters and distributed them after prayers. Old people in their sixties and seventies helped as well. People distributed it everywhere they could—in taxis, in the subway, in the streets, in schools and universities, in private companies and government offices."

Mahfouz seemed genuinely touched by the massive reactions she received from her first video, citing an avalanche of e-mails and phone calls.

"Everyone who talks to me, talks as if I'm his sister or his daughter or his mother. I felt like I am truly the daughter of Egypt. I felt that I am your daughter and you are concerned about me. This is the most beautiful thing I have ever felt in my life."

More than anything else, she sounded confident. Her faith in her people had been partially restored by what she had witnessed that week. She seemed to know exactly what was going to happen the next day, offering a remarkably accurate prediction of how the revolution would progress.

"We'll defend each other as one. We'll come prepared to spend the whole day, or two days or even three days . . . no matter what they do to us, we will not leave until our demands are met," she said. "I'll see you all tomorrow at Moustafa Mahmoud Mosque. I'll be there at 2 P.M. sharp. Don't be late and don't forget to bring a flag of Egypt with you. This flag is our shield and this is our country . . . tomorrow I'll be waiting for you guys."

———

On January 24, Kassem was fielding a steady stream of phone calls from journalists and diplomats seeking some sort of prediction or prognosis for the following day. His stock response: "I don't know. It could be the big one or it could fizzle out. All I can tell you is that the country is volatile. It could happen at any moment. It could happen in a year or in five, but either way this regime has taken things to the point where an explosion is inevitable."

Khalil spent the lead-up to the twenty-fifth exchanging e-mails with the anonymous administrator of the "We Are All Khaled Saieed" Facebook page, which had become one of the main planning hubs. Khalil had actually met Wael Ghonim socially about a year before; both were members of the relatively small fraternity of Arab World IT professionals. But at the time, Khalil said he had no idea he was communicating with him.

Khalil also reached out via e-mail to a Brazilian political cartoonist named Carlos Latuff, a known supporter of international revolutionary causes. Latuff immediately provided half a dozen sketches that were incorporated into the prerevolutionary iconography. One of the most memorable cartoons features the unmistakable image of young Khaled Saieed in his gray hooded sweatshirt, dangling a tiny struggling Hosni Mubarak by the collar of his suit.

Organizers cleverly chose the day's main demands from the bubbling stew of modern Egyptian grievances, settling on a short list of core issues that would resonate widely across society.

- Disbanding the current Parliament and holding new and legitimate elections
- Instituting a two-term limit for the presidency
- Canceling the Emergency Laws and dismissing Interior Minister Habib al-Adly
- Raising the minimum wage to LE1200 (around $220) per month and establishing unemployment benefits

Hamdeen Sabahi, the lifelong opposition politician and former independent MP, said the Tunisian example could have the effect of embarrassing Egyptian citizens and political leaders into action.

"Now political powers will feel that they're not doing their duty if they don't move," Sabahi said in an interview. "Our regime is not less corrupt than their regime and our people are not less capable than the Tunisians."

The Security State, no doubt equally mindful of the Tunisian example, made it clear that they intended to keep things on a short leash. The Interior Ministry's directorate for Cairo Security issued an ominous statement warning that "The security apparatus will deal firmly and decisively with any attempt to break the law," while al-Adly himself said he had issued orders to "arrest any persons expressing their views illegally."

Since Egypt under Mubarak banned demonstrations without prior permission, and no such permits were issued (or even applied for most likely) this meant that any protests anywhere, no matter how small or peaceful, could potentially be targeted.

Al-Adly, unknowingly entering his final week as head of a functioning police state, sounded supremely confident. In his final pre–January 25 public comments, he dismissed the "Facebook phenomenon," saying, "I tell the public that this Facebook call comes from the youth," he said in an *Al-Ahram* interview. "Youth street action has no impact and security is capable of deterring any acts outside the law." He then magnanimously added that his forces would allow "stationary protests held for limited periods of time."

Of the major opposition players, only the Muslim Brotherhood announced it would not formally participate, although it also wouldn't prevent its members from joining as individuals.

Mohammed al-Beltagy, the former Brotherhood MP, explained in a newspaper interview that the Brotherhood's decision to sit out January 25 was motivated by a desire to outmaneuver the regime. If the Brotherhood participated en masse, al-Beltagy stated, the government would have controlled the narrative and painted the events as one more power play by the menacing, bearded Islamist hordes.

"We don't want it to be a fight between the ruling regime and the Muslim Brotherhood, because it is really a fight between the ruling regime and all the people," he said.

In retrospect, whether or not you believe al-Beltagy's

explanation of the famously opaque Brotherhood decision-making process, the group's choice to "sit out" January 25 proved to be one of the best legacies of that day. Egypt's non-Islamist forces needed to prove (perhaps to themselves as well) that they could marshal mass numbers into the streets without the help of the Brotherhood's legendary grassroots machinery. And ordinary apolitical Egyptians who feared the Brotherhood's power needed to see that this wasn't coming from the Islamist camp. The way things eventually played out, with the Brotherhood formally joining several days into an already robust popular uprising, turned out to be a tremendous boost to the credibility, perception, and confidence of the revolutionaries.

I was originally scheduled to travel to Dubai on January 25; my wife Rola was already there waiting for me. Hearing all the rumblings and mindful of Tunisia, I decided to delay the trip by a day or so, just to see what happened. By the end of the day, it was clear that I wasn't going anywhere. It was still way too early to predict where all this was going, but something unprecedented was happening.

Organizers originally called for crowds to gather outside the Interior Ministry, near Tahrir Square. On the surface, that seemed like a tactical mistake. Gathering in the tightly confined urban space of Lazoghly Square would enable the Central Security troops to practice their well-honed tactics of bottling up protest groups with overwhelming numbers. Anyone gathering in Lazoghly would be easily surrounded, and anyone seeking to join the protest in progress would be just as easily prevented from approaching.

The Interior Ministry plan turned out to be a clever ruse; at about 10:30 in the morning, the word went out through Twitter and Facebook about a whole new set of gathering points and contact numbers.

The turnout exceeded all expectations; from the start, it was clear that this was, at the very least, the largest demonstration Egypt had witnessed in years. I spent the day moving throughout downtown Cairo, trying to keep track of a dizzying set of fast-moving events. A series of scattered protests moved through different parts of the city, growing in strength as they joined up with other groups and induced onlookers and residents to join in.

Near the Ramsis Hilton, about a block from Tahrir Square and the Egyptian Museum, I followed a group of about two dozen protesters waving the green flags of the Wafd Party. This was itself a small surprise since the Wafd—which had a proud history as an opposition force in the days of the monarchy—had become in modern times a bit of a joke. Under Mubarak in particular, the Wafd became symbolic of the tame and co-opted pseudo-opposition which existed only to capture a few parliament seats and foster the illusion of a true democracy. Its leaders were literally indistinguishable from government ministers and its platform consisted of little more than a belief that the Wafd's set of autocratic eighty-year-olds should be running the country instead of the NDP's set of autocratic eighty-year-olds.

If the Wafd was indeed taking to the streets and calling for the fall of the regime, it meant one of two things: either they had finally broken with the regime in a meaningful way, or its leaders had astutely judged the post-Tunisia political winds and decided to save face and get on the right side of history. The Wafd Party contingent's presence was also notable since this represented the absolute last time during the entire revolution that I saw any signs or flags from any one Egyptian party, movement, or faction. From that point on, the protests—seemingly by a sort of unspoken groupthink—became an unaffiliated mass movement.

Throughout the day, different groups of protesters flowed organically through downtown Cairo, many of them meeting little resistance. There was a carnival atmosphere, and protesters saluted each other and joined forces, moving through the city with no set plan—only an unspoken understanding that something new was happening and that they would all eventually meet in Tahrir.

The black-clad riot troops of Central Security dutifully deployed in their usual overwhelming waves. But for the first time in recent memory the troops seemed potentially outnumbered by the protesters, who simply pushed through their ranks. The Central Security cadres looked strikingly unprepared and completely miserable; they weren't used to a fair fight.

———

The security troops also seemed to be operating under orders, at first, to deploy a soft touch. Perhaps out of concern over how the Tunisian uprising had captured imaginations across the Middle East, authorities seemed concerned to avoid a major public crackdown. At the beginning of the day on the twenty-fifth, the Central Security forces deployed without their usual batons and riot shields, locking arms to form a human barrier to pen in demonstrators. That tactic quickly proved to be almost comically ineffective.

The first real physical confrontations I witnessed were outside the Supreme Court downtown—a common flash point since it sits adjacent to the Lawyers Syndicate and Journalists Syndicate, which are both longtime nerve centers for protests and activism. The two neighboring professional syndicates are both symbolic of how opposition politics worked for years under Mubarak. Both, in their time, served as hotbeds of government opposition; but both also clearly demonstrate how Mubarak's forces would allow limited "steam vent" protests to express public frustration without actually threatening to change anything.

For years you could say pretty much anything you wanted outside either syndicate building, far more than you ever could say in Tunisia, Syria, or Libya—as long as you didn't try to move from your spot. The Lawyers Syndicate in particular had a walled-in courtyard with a front gate that served nicely as a natural choke point to keep protests inside. At the Journalists Syndicate around the corner, protesters frequently gathered on the wide steps of the building's entrance, where they would also be surrounded by riot cops and penned in place. Most of the time, Central Security forces were able to keep matters so effectively bottled up that traffic would keep flowing past the buildings, with passing drivers barely noticing one more noisy distraction.

It was a solid plan and it worked for literally decades. But it was entirely built around the concept of over-whelming security numbers—that there would always be more police than protesters. January 25, on the block of Ramsis Street that contained both syndicates and the Supreme Court, was the first time I had ever witnessed where the numbers weren't heavily in the government's favor.

"All day you had this sense of euphoria," said Mohamed El Dahshan, who had returned to Egypt one day earlier after helping monitor the referendum on independence for South Sudan. "It was like, 'Fuck it, there's a lot of us!' No more getting cordoned by a measly couple hundred Central Security people . . . You would walk with people you recognize, lose them, find some others, and walk and chant with them."

Across the river, on the Giza side, the blogger Mahmoud Salem (Sandmonkey) started his day outside the Moustafa Mahmoud Mosque—a central hub in the commercial district of Mohandessin. At about 12:30 in the afternooon he was sitting inside Cilantro, an upscale coffee shop across Arab League Street from the mosque, waiting for some friends to arrive. Suddenly four police officers entered and started demanding IDs and detain-

ing all veiled women and bearded men—basically anyone who looked like an Islamist. The government clearly
still thought the primary threat that day would come from
the fundamentalist ranks. "They left my group alone because we looked like froufrou upper-class Cilantro people," Salem said.

Eventually he ended up in a five-hundred-strong march
that tried to cross the Nile and head toward Tahrir. But
Central Security had effectively cut the city in two, blocking multiple bridges in the center of the city. Unable to
cross the Galaa Bridge, Salem and his group moved north
to the October 6 Bridge, but found that also blocked by
overwhelming security numbers. In a moment of pure inspiration, Salem found a Nile-side fisherman with a motorboat and gave him LE150 (about $25) on the spot to
deliver him and a few friends across the river and right up
to the entrance to Tahrir Square.

"We called it the Egyptian Freedom Flotilla," Salem
said, laughing proudly. "There was even an Egyptian flag
on the side of the motorboat!"

Back at the Supreme Court, after a bit of back-and-forth
shoving, the crowds started to overwhelm the police, who
scrambled to keep up. For a while, it was almost playful;
groups of police and protesters would race to reach this or
that intersection in time, often running side by side and
jostling for position.

One group of marchers, moving through the Boulaq
area, seemed to make a point of recruiting as they went.

Protesters openly appealed to the sidewalk gawkers to join and chanted, "Raise your voice/he that shouts won't die!" (It rhymes in Arabic.)

"Join us, you won't go to jail," one young man shouted to a group of youths watching from the sidewalk. "Don't be afraid. The fear is what keeps us from changing."

The dominant chant, the first time I'd heard it in years of covering Egyptian protests, was a direct import from Tunisia: *"Al-shaab yureed isqat al-nizam* (The people demand the fall of the regime)."

Even among those who didn't join in, there seemed to be a high degree of emotional support for the marchers. A chubby young mother carrying a wriggling toddler gave the protesters a thumbs-up. Down the block, a grandmother gleefully clapped and chanted along.

In a powerful moment, a three-hundred-strong group of protestors came across another, larger, group of demonstrators marching the opposite direction along the Corniche near Tahrir Square. The two groups embraced amid raucous cheers and started marching together.

All across the city, similar scenes were playing out. Maha Elgamal, the ElBaradei volunteer, recalls marching along the Corniche on the western bank of the Nile in the district of Agouza in the early evening. "We saw this army coming towards us and thought they were Central Security coming to crush us. It turned out it was a huge crowd of more protesters coming from Imbaba. It was dark and we thought they were the police and they thought we were the police! We all hugged each other and cheered."

At one point, more than a thousand people stood outside a building along the Nile belonging to Mubarak's ruling National Democratic Party and chanted "illegitimate" and "Oh Mubarak, your plane is waiting for you."

It was just the first of dozens of scenes that many Egyptians never thought they would witness. Even after Tunisia, it was difficult to imagine the Egyptian people truly rebelling against authority in this kind of mass numbers.

But the sight of Tunisians driving the similarly entrenched Ben Ali from power had seemingly unblocked something in the psyches of the protesters. Now that they knew it was possible, people couldn't wait to get on with their own liberation.

There was also, it must be noted, a certain level of brotherly Arab competitiveness on display. Egyptians have always prided themselves on being the cultural and political leaders of the Arab world—even in the last few decades when that boast began to ring rather hollow. The sight of the Tunisians (the Tunisians, of all people!) accomplishing what Egyptians couldn't do had rekindled that semidormant sense of Egyptian competitive pride—as if liberation was some sort of African Cup match.

Mahmoud "Sandmonkey" Salem, frames the matter rather indelicately as "the small penis theory" of Middle Eastern politics. "Machismo played a big part of it," he insists. "Egyptians looked at Tunisia and said, 'Wait that's possible? And you're just fucking Tunisia! We're Egypt!'"

Other protesters expressed similar sentiments in more

delicate terms. "Tunisia has encouraged a lot of people. I was one of those people who never got into politics," said one woman in her mid-fifties who declined to give her name.

"The Tunisians never used to protest. They were even more tightly controlled than we are," said Sobhi Mohammed Hassan. "Now look at them."

Downtown, a few yards away from where demonstrators were clashing with riot police outside the Supreme Court, a young protester seemed to capture the brotherly competitiveness best.

"The Tunisians have become better than us. They're real men," Ahmed Eid told me.

Eid was a classic profile of young Egyptian frustration. An educated middle-class youth, he saw no hope and no future for himself under the current system. Despite holding a law school degree, he was still unemployed after graduating four years earlier. In Egyptian social mathematics, this also meant he was still living with his parents with virtually no hope of ever getting married (which probably meant no hope of ever having sex) and actually starting his life. He was basically one of the characters from *Cultural Film.*

"We've been silent and gone hungry for a long time," Eid said. "If we continue like this, we will change things, we just have to commit."

As one thousand protestors jostled with riot police outside the Supreme Court downtown, on a deserted stretch of 26 July Street, a young family—middle-aged man and woman with a boy who looked about nine years old—walked arm in arm down the middle of the street gleefully chanting, "Down with Hosni Mubarak!"

It became apparent that something different was happening here than the usual semiannual bursts of public frustration. The anger and the desire for change had metastasized. Whatever anyone says about the Egyptian revolution, it wasn't just "the youth" that brought Mubarak down. The youth led the way, for sure, often showing courage that their elders had long since surrendered. But from the very start it encompassed people at all age levels, including innumerable two- and three-generation families, all adding to the protest lines.

One woman in her mid-forties, who declined to give her name, said she had never before gotten involved in politics. But on the twenty-fifth she came out with her two teenage sons, "to show them that it's possible to demonstrate peacefully for change."

At about three in the afternoon, the crowds converged on Tahrir Square, the massive public space on the edge of downtown that's the traditional heart of the city. The protesters filled up more than half the square; that's when the riot police started hauling out the heavier tactics—including baton charges, water cannons, and tear gas.

In a surreal interlude, at the Talaat Harb Street entrance to Tahrir Square, there was a mass of protesters and Central Security cadres—all gagging on the same tear gas. Despite the violence on display, the day contained its share of dark comedy. There was the sight of now-desperate Egyptian riot police throwing rocks *back* at protesters.

A tense standoff reigned for hours. Several times, the riot police scattered the crowd with choking tear-gas volleys, but the protesters kept regrouping and coming back for more. In the midst of conflict, there were numerous moments of détente and even sympathy between the two warring sides. Many of the Central Security soldiers and commanders seemed to understand the frustrations of the protesters, and many of the protestors seemed to understand that the Central Security was the most immediate problem but not the real problem. Mohab Wahby, the young development specialist, recalls a rather civil negotiation with a Central Security officer who told him, "I understand your anger, but what can I do? These are my orders."

As news of the clashes spread, the various protest groups began converging on Tahrir to provide reinforcements. Just before 4:00 P.M. just as the police were potentially starting to turn the tide, a thousand-strong march rushed in from the direction of Abdin with a huge roar, adding fresh numbers and momentum to the protesters.

Throughout the day Twitter proved to be a crucial platform for both organization and real-time reports from the street. Protesters not only knew what was happening blocks away or across town, they were also tracking in real time what was happening across Egypt. News that protests in the canal city of Suez had turned into particularly violent clashes rippled through Tahrir like a current. But Twitter service abruptly stopped working for most people at about 4:30 in the afternoon, prompting speculation that it had been blocked. Within hours,

tech-savvy tweeters were distributing instructions on how to install proxies to evade the blockage.

In the midst of the maelstrom, I witnessed a goose-bump-inducing moment. A fresh volley of tear gas had once again scattered the crowds from the heart of Tahrir Square. A young woman in her late twenties climbed atop a raised platform in the middle of the square—part of the ventilation system for the subway running underneath Tahrir. The young woman defiantly waved a huge Egyptian flag as the tear gas swirled; the crowd roared and rallied around her.

As evening approached, "The discussion became, 'Do we stay or not?' People were saying, 'If we leave, we'll never take the square again.' Then people started getting blankets and food," said Mohamed El Dahshan.

Fresh bodies began flocking to the square, having heard the news of its occupation by protesters. Someone brought a microphone and speaker system and the speeches began. Political and cultural leaders like Alaa Al Aswany, author of the aforementioned novel *The Yacoubian Building*, started appearing on the scene and determination hardened around the idea of an open-ended sit-in.

The protesters managed to hold onto Tahrir for about nine hours that day. At about one in the morning, when the crowds had thinned a bit, police violently cleared the square using volleys of tear gas and baton charges.

"We were really getting into sleep mode, and then suddenly here comes the cavalry," El Dahshan said.

He and others fled through the side streets of downtown with Central Security chasing them and throwing rocks. As he was catching his breath and regrouping with friends outside the famed downtown café called Horreya, El Dahshan witnessed something that made him realize the battle wasn't going to be won that day. "Around two A.M., I saw a police paddy wagon stop and drop off about a dozen guys in civilian clothes with sticks," he said. "I didn't stick around for long after that."

As they were being run out of Tahrir, one group of protesters made a brief, disastrous attempt to invade the grounds of the NDP headquarters, which are tucked away behind the Egyptian Museum at the northern edge of the square. They were overrun by police and savagely beaten, said Mohab Wahby, who witnessed the scene from above on the October 6 Bridge.

The day ended in defeat for the protesters, but the turnout had already surprised all sides and officially taken Mubarak's regime into uncharted waters.

"By the end of that night, I naïvely thought we had already won and that Mubarak was gone," Wahby recalled. "You went home and you were thinking, 'I'm coming back tomorrow no matter what.'"

Organizers, sensing the initiative was on their side, called for Friday January 28 to be a massive "Day of Rage" protest. Pamphlets widely distributed among protesters the following day clearly conveyed that sense of unprecedented confidence and momentum.

"We have started an uprising with the will of the people, the people who have suffered for thirty years under oppression, injustice, and poverty," read the Arabic-language text. "Egyptians have proven today that they are

capable of taking freedom by force and destroying despotism."

But despite the day's successes, it would still have been impossible to predict just where things would go and it was still, frankly, difficult to imagine Mubarak's twenty-nine-year reign collapsing. What brought Ben Ali down in Tunisia wasn't a one-day mass protest, but a solid month of uncontrollable political activity throughout the country. As of dawn on January 26, it was still an open question whether Egyptians could generate enough sustained pressure and willpower to produce the same result.

8

Safwat's Last Stand

The final days of the Mubarak regime featured a multitude of generally shameless, desperate, and tone-deaf reactions and tactics by the government. But the low point that stands out was a bizarre, hastily convened press conference on Thursday, January 27, at the headquarters of the National Democratic Party just outside of Tahrir Square.

Egypt had just witnessed its largest antigovernment protests in a generation and more unrest was planned. The interim had seen scattered clashes that crucially kept the shock troops of Central Security on the run and constantly responding. Protest organizers were calling for a massive turnout the following day, and everybody was feeling fired up by the events of the twenty-fifth. The world had taken notice and big-time correspondents were flooding in; everyone seemed to know the next forty-eight hours or so would be pivotal. Clearly some sort of government response was called for.

Into this breach shuffled the diminutive figure of Safwat al-Sherif, the NDP's Secretary General and head of the Shoura Council, the appointed, rubber-stamp upper house of Parliament. It was perfect; Hosni Mubarak's government couldn't have chosen a more appropriate spokesman. Al-Sherif was a quintessential regime crony and former Information Minister whose ties to Egypt's military rulers date back to Gamal Abdel Nasser in the 1960s. With his jet-black dye job and pancake makeup, the guy looked the part of a sinister fascist reptile.

Al-Sherif was the kind of guy who always seemed to be lurking behind a strongman: the oily apparatchik. He would have fit in seamlessly in Mayor Richard Daley's Chicago machine as a hatchet-man ward boss who lasted for generations and survived multiple shakeups and reorganizations.

Indeed al-Sherif had endured through several eras, surviving as his contemporaries were purged. In the late '90s and early 2000s, he was part of a trio of powerful ministers regarded as the government within the government. Al-Sherif was Information Minister, Youseff Wali was Deputy Prime Minister and Agriculture Minister—a quietly crucial and influential post—and Kamal El Shazli, another archetypal regime fixer who was parodied in *The Yacoubian Building*, was Minister of Parliamentary Affairs (translation: enforcing internal discipline and steamrolling the opposition on the Parliament floor).

Their power went largely unchecked until the political

emergence of Gamal Mubarak in 2001. Suddenly the papers were full of chatter about a struggle between Gamal's new guard and Safwat's entrenched old-school cronies. Much of that was NDP-generated hype to burnish Gamal Mubarak's credentials as a young reformer, but either way, Safwat and his clique were eventually put to pasture. Wali and El Shazli were dramatically demoted, but Safwat managed to get kicked upstairs to an emeritus position while keeping his hand in the game. He was regarded as locked in a seemingly never-ending power struggle with Gamal's faction.

So it was that Safwat al-Sherif, the eternal and indispensible crony, was summoned to make his last public performance. He didn't disappoint either, delivering a medley of NDP's greatest hits—a fifteen-minute string of clichés that didn't begin to approach the reality on the streets. Al-Sherif hailed the achievements of the NDP and Mubarak's government—emphasizing socialized health care and education and the subsidized food and fuel. He made vague promises of "widening political participation" while simultaneously dismissing the street protesters as "a few thousands" and said that a loud minority shouldn't be able to disrupt the lives of the happy majority. He never mentioned Tunisia once but made an apparent reference in saying, "We don't imitate other countries. We are Egypt!"

At least five times, he said some variation of "The Party has its hand on the pulse of the youth." Al-Sherif concluded with a quote that should be engraved on his headstone: "Egypt is stable, God willing."

It was, to put it bluntly, a delusional performance, seemingly broadcast from a parallel reality. The first week of the revolution proved how vulnerable Mubarak's police state was physically, once faced with a sufficiently large and motivated foe. On January 27, al-Sherif proved to any remaining doubters that the regime was ideologically and creatively spent as well.

Less than twenty-four hours later, the room that al-Sherif spoke from was in flames, and the historic Egyptian revolution was in full swing. If al-Sherif and his fellow NDP elders truly had their "hand on the pulse" of the people, they would have headed to the airport that night, because the people were baying for their blood.

On the twenty-seventh, the assembled crowd of journalists walked out laughing at what had just been witnessed. But later that night came proof that the Mubarak regime still had some teeth behind the detached bluster.

Around midnight on Thursday the 27th, Internet service slowed to a crawl and then stopped working completely, prompting a frantic series of calls. My old friend Issandr "Arabist" El Amrani, actually called me from Tunisia, where he was covering the aftermath of that revolution, to tell me about the shutdown. Hossam Hamalawy, the veteran hard-core socialist activist known online as Arabawy and a veteran of the *Cairo Times,* informed me of a rumor that men in military fatigues had been spotted deploying in Tahrir Square. Too nervous to sleep, I took a stroll to Giza Square, near my apartment, then a 1:00 A.M. taxi ride to Tahrir just to check things out and found nothing beyond the usual Central Security paddy wagons.

While the government made its preparatory moves in advance of the showdown, the other side wasn't sitting idle. Ahmad Abdalla, a young movie director, spent this period between the storms volunteering to help the hundreds of protesters who had been rounded up by police on the twenty-fifth. The Hisham Mubarak Law Center, a venerable human rights NGO, was one of the nerve centers for tracking the detainees, and Abdalla, in coordination with the HMLC, crisscrossed the city offering comfort to those coming out of custody. Often a group of detainees would be released from a district prosecutor's office bewildered and penniless; Abdalla and other volunteers would meet them with blankets, food, clothing, and some cash to get home.

"We went to Tawheed wa Nur [a popular department store chain run by Islamists] because it was cheaper," Abdalla said. "When we told them we were getting supplies for the protest detainees, they loved us. We were buying seventy tracksuits, one hundred blankets, that kind of thing."

Mahmoud "Sandmonkey" Salem chose a different strategy; he and a group of friends "decided that we were going to be the tear-gas-catching squad."

Heading to the local sporting goods store, they stocked up on goalie gloves and soccer shin pads to put on their forearms. The idea was that when Central Security fired tear-gas cannisters into the protesters' ranks, Salem and his buddies would pounce on the hot metal cylinders and throw them far away from the crowds. They bought swim goggles, bandanas, spray bottles, and lots of vinegar (to counteract the effects of tear gas). Salem found a paint supply store and acquired several industrial-strength gas masks. In anticipation of the looming communications shutdown, they set up safe houses and communal gathering points.

Mohamed El Dahshan spent the night of the twenty-seventh calling friends in other countries—waking them up in some cases—and putting everyone on alert. "Tomorrow we want to be able to get information out," he told them. "I'm counting on your guys to relay information because they're planning something nasty."

Asmaa Mahfouz, the April 6 Movement activist whose YouTube videos had touched so many, posted a new video message late on January 26. This one started on a celebratory note, with Mahfouz chanting, "The people want the fall of the regime! That's what we were all shouting yesterday. There were thousands upon thousands. I couldn't count them all. Demonstrations from every direction, the security couldn't control the sheer numbers. What we learned yesterday was that power belongs to the people, not to the thugs. Power is in unity, not division. Yesterday we truly lived the best moments of our lives. . . . The government keeps saying that we are a chaotic people and a revolution will lead to chaos. But yesterday we were truly one hand, concerned for

each other. Yesterday not even one girl was harassed, even among the thousands. No one stole anything. No fights broke out. We were defending each other. . . . This is the Egyptian people we have always dreamed of. I can now say that I am proud to be Egyptian. I want to kiss every Egyptian's forehead and say, 'Thank you for being Egyptian.'"

With the celebratory self-congratulations out of the way, she turned to future tasks, making it clear that the victories of the twenty-fifth would only have meaning if they were followed by increased and sustained public pressure.

"We have a long road ahead, but not too long. Just a few more days, a few more days united. A few more days knowing that the power belongs to the people and our strength is in our unity . . . right now each of you must knock on your neighbors, door by door. Tell them the uprising is here. Tell them we'll no longer live like animals and beggars. . . . Every day we're out there, they get weaker. Go onto public transport and tell everyone. On Friday after prayers we march from the mosques and the churches, and we'll call on the people to join us. The numbers on the twenty-fifth were huge, but still not enough. Everyone go through your mobile phone contacts and call or text people. They're trying to shut down Facebook and Twitter. So what can we do? There's no solution but to take to the streets."

As she accelerated toward her conclusion, Mahfouz became overtaken with emotion. Her voice cracked, tears visibly welling up in her eyes, and she began to stammer a bit. What started eight days earlier as an angry and disgusted young woman literally challenging her countrymen to demonstrate basic courage and dignity had become something new and hopeful. The people Mahfouz had so little faith in had proven themselves to her in a major way. It was almost too much to believe.

"Our dream is here. It just needs a little more patience . . . Long live Egypt! That was our unified chant yesterday. Our dreams are coming true!"

With the tears starting to flow freely, Mahfouz said, "On Friday, after prayers, we will not give up this land! We will not leave it to the thieves. We will take our country back. Please be there on Friday."

9

The Fall of the Police State

Much has been made of the near-obsessive dedication to nonviolence on the part of the Tahrir square protesters. For the most part, that's true. From the very start, one of the dominant chants from the protesters was *salmeya*, or peaceful.

But let's pause now to acknowledge and honor the fact that Egypt's nonviolent revolution wouldn't have happened without some people who were willing to be extremely violent at times. Over a four-day period, a hard-core cadre of protesters confronted and physically shattered the Egyptian police state—overwhelming the shock troops of the Interior Ministry's Central Security riot police. It was only after that vanguard had been physically destroyed and demoralized that the real revolution could begin.

Most popular uprisings boil down to very simple mathematics at some point. First, the people overwhelm the traditional security forces. At that point it becomes a question of whether the government in charge has the will to order its military to attack civilians, and then whether the military is willing to follow those orders. If both are willing, then you get Tiananmen Square; if not, then you get Tunisia.

It was on January 28 that Egyptians forced that dilemma onto Mubarak's government by violently defeating Egypt's Interior Ministry, essentially stripping away Mubarak's armor and forcing him to genuinely deal with his people for the first time in decades. I witnessed scenes of incredible violence on January 28, with protesters using military-style organization and tactics to harass and pressure the police until they collapsed.

Across the city, protesters and security forces were making their final preparations. First thing in the morning, Mohamed El Dahshan headed to the local sporting goods store, just as Salem and others had done the day before. One of the random peripheral economic benefits of the Egyptian revolution seems to have been a massive spike in demand for swim goggles.

"I told the store owner, 'I want cheap transparent swim goggles,'" El Dahshan said. "He laughed and replied, 'Oh for the revolution? Well, all your friends bought this kind over here.'"

The day started with the final step of the government communications blackout. At about nine in the morning, all cell phones in the country went dead. I was on a rooftop in the west bank Nile-side district of Agouza preparing to be interviewed for the BBC, when one by one everybody's cell phone signal died, including those with foreign Sim cards. A relative who saw me on television minutes later said I looked nervous and rattled—and I was. It was an intimidating move, not simply because the government chose to do it, but because of what it implied was coming next.

It didn't matter. The communications shutdown came far too late to blunt the day's events. Protest organizers basically bypassed the idea of coordination and communication altogether and just told people "Protest everywhere and don't stop." The government's desperate move to strangle the flow of information didn't hinder the demonstrators, and it didn't stop the journalists from communicating what they witnessed to the world.

One of the most remarkable things about the January 28 Day of Rage is that it took place inside an unprecedented information vacuum. On the twenty-fifth, half the protesters seemed to be constantly on their smartphones, either tweeting or checking for news on what was happening across the country. But on the twenty-eighth, nobody knew what was happening anywhere else—not even on the other side of the river. If anything, the information vacuum may have ended up sharpening the wills of the demonstrators. With no idea of the situation anywhere else, protestors had no choice but to fight like hell for whatever public patch of ground they were standing on— and then fight their way through to the next patch of ground.

All through that day and deep into the night, Cairo reverted to a surreal word-of-mouth storyteller society. If you were walking on the street and you saw protestors coming in the other direction, you asked them where they were coming from and what the situation was like there. It was intimate and even pleasant.

Several participants in the pivotal January twenty-eighth protests speculated that the government's blanket communications shutdown backfired badly—providing that final motivation to draw unprecedented numbers out of their homes. Like so many of the government's decisions in those final days (really in the prior year or so) the move to strangle communications came too late and ended up accomplishing the opposite of its intended effect.

"There was no Internet and no cell phones. That more than anything brought people into the streets," said Maha Elgamal. "If you wanted to know what was happening, you had to go out. If you were a mother scared for her son, and wanted to make sure he was all right, you had to go out. But even on the twenty-eighth, it was impossible to predict that a revolution was coming. I was still working on the assumption that we were five years away."

Rawya Rageh, the Al Jazeera International correspondent, covered January 28 from Alexandria and observed an identical phenomenon. The lack of information produced a huge pool of curious onlookers, who were then either emboldened by the numbers around them or enraged by the violence they witnessed.

"Even those who had no interest in the revolution

headed out to see what was going on. Then when they saw the brutality, they joined the protests," Rageh said.

All across the country, nonparticipants were being drawn into the fray. Hisham Kassem, despite years spent as a human rights activist and a troublemaking independent publisher, rarely attended public protests.

"I actually hate demonstrations," he said with a grin. "It's just a lot of noise, and I consider myself more of a strategic man."

But on the morning of the twenty-eighth, he decided to set aside his prejudices and head to the streets. "The time had come. It was the defining moment. We were at the point where every citizen who didn't step out would be complicit."

Several hours later, Kassem would reach another turning point. He was in the midst of a chaotic tear-gas and baton battle with Central Security moving back and forth across the October 6 Bridge—a massive span that stretches across the Nile, crossing the island of Zamalek, and moves past the Egyptian Museum and NDP head-quarters at the northern entrance to Tahrir. At that point, Kassem was chanting slogans and helping the injured, but not playing an offensive role in the conflict. An armored van approached them and a soldier emerged from the van's rooftop hatch and started indiscriminately firing buck-shot into the crowd. "The people on my right and my left were all shot with pellets," Kassem said. "At that point, I joined the rock throwers."

———

I started walking with an approximately eight-thousand-strong march starting from Moustafa Mahmoud Mosque in the Mohandessin district, across the Nile from Tahrir. From the start it was obvious that the turnout would be beyond all previous numbers, and that the protesters had a significant amount of passive societal support. One indication of the size of the crowds that day: several people I've interviewed—including Mahmoud "Sandmonkey" Salem, Wael Khalil, and Ahmad Abdalla—all started marching from Moustafa Mahmoud as well, and we never met at any point during the day. It was too chaotic and there were simply too many people.

"People were coming from everywhere," Khalil said. "It was like, 'Oh my God, it's happening!'"

The anti-Mubarak chants started as soon as the noon prayers finished. Marchers completely filled both sides of Batal Ahmed Abdez Aziz Street, a major six-lane artery, extending for several blocks. Crucially, many of the nonmarching area residents expressed their own support. I saw several people waving flags from their windows, and an elderly woman in her housecoat flashing the V for victory sign from her balcony. The marchers constantly chanted "Enzel!" (come down) to draw out the fence-sitters while one young man took a more aggressive approach, yelling at camera-phone gawkers, "Stop filming and join! Take a stand for once."

Immediately striking was not just the size of the crowds, but the diversity on display. After years of protests populated by all the usual suspects, now the crowds were filled with unrecognizable faces.

There was a paunchy white-haired man, holding hands and chanting with his middle-aged veiled wife. They looked like average middle-aged Egyptians, but spoke like people whose patience had absolutely run out. "We don't want Mubarak anymore. It's time for him to go," the man said with intensity. When asked if he was concerned about violence today, he literally shrugged. "I'm not worried at all. I'm ready to die."

Some of the protesters came clearly primed for a fight, wearing swim goggles or carrying onions and vinegar-soaked cloths, all in hopes of fending off tear-gas attacks. But the overall mood was jubilant and studiously nonviolent. At one point, some hothead protester started vandalizing a roadside McDonald's advertisement; the others quickly dragged him away, shouting "peaceful." It was an impressive moment, one which displayed the kind of spontaneous and sincere groupthink that would make Egypt's protesters such a potent force.

The march turned east onto Tahrir Street, an eventual corridor across Zamalek Island and directly into Tahrir Square. Police up until this point had kept to the edges of the crowd, simply monitoring and making no attempt to hinder the marchers' movements. But other parts of the country had already descended into revolutionary bedlam. In Giza Square (where a newly-returned Mohammed ElBaradei had joined the protests), the tear gas started flying as soon as the protesters started to move. In Alexandria, security didn't even wait for prayers at

downtown's Qaed Ibrahim Mosque to finish before attacking.

"People were still raising their heads from the prayer
mats when the tear gas started," said Rawya Rageh. "Literally they were saying '*Sallamu Aleykum wa Rahmat
Allah*,' [the traditional prayer-ending phrase] and before
they could finish the sentence, tear gas—tear gas—tear
gas."

El Dahshan, the economist and blogger, was coming
in from Heliopolis in a taxi taking the elevated October 6
flyover—which gave him a bird's-eye view of a city in
convulsions. Above Ramsis Square, basically the western edge of downtown Cairo, El Dahshan said he could
see a "full-blown rock war" taking place below. "It was
more of a riot than a protest," he said. Farther along the
flyover, which eventually passes just behind the Egyptian Museum, El Dahshan said he spotted the police station in the district of Ezbekia—with "soldiers and officers
standing on the roof, throwing rocks down at the protesters surrounding the station."

Back on Tahrir Street in Mohandessin, the group
continued peacefully, completely oblivious of what
was happening elsewhere, thanks to the communications
shutdown. It wasn't until reaching Galaa Square on the
western bank of the Nile that the police decided to put a
stop to things. The Galaa Bridge is a small affair, maybe
two hundred meters across. It leads to a short stretch of
road that crosses an uninhabited part of Zamalek, brack-
eted by a large public garden and a sports club to the
south and the expansive grounds of the Cairo Opera

House to the north. Beyond that was the long Kasr al-Nil Bridge, the final gateway to Tahrir Square.

The security forces wisely chose the Galaa Bridge (a natural bottleneck and choke point) as their first line of defense. Once the bridge came into sight, it became clear why the police had let the march go so far unimpeded. They were waiting in force ahead, with a thick phalanx of riot cops engulfing the mouth of the bridge. Behind the troops, four large paddy wagons were parked side by side, completely blocking the bridge itself. As the crowd closed in, the inevitable shoving matches began on the front lines, but the police quickly hauled out the tear gas and blanketed the area with massive volleys of acrid white chemical smoke.

The deployment of the tear gas was almost comically indiscriminate. The canisters flew everywhere. Clouds of gas engulfed the Giza Sheraton, the five-star hotel that overlooks Galaa Square. Curious tourists on the balconies scrambled inside as the gas enveloped them. (At one point, probably between my second and third face full of gas, I was seized by the stress-induced urge to stop by the hotel and ask residents how they were enjoying their vacation.)

Several sizzling-hot gas canisters landed on the concrete tarmac grounds of a nearby petrol station, where a team of terrified employees with water hoses sprang into action to douse each new incoming shell. One protester told me he believed the police were deliberately targeting the gas station "so it explodes and they can blame it on us."

One shell landed on the seventh floor balcony of a nearby apartment building, starting a small fire. Comically, another shell landed inside the cab of a riot police paddy wagon parked nearby, setting that on fire as well. The flames spread from the driver's area of the truck and consumed the whole vehicle, as protesters cheered and laughed.

For about two hours, starting at about two in the afternoon, the conflict flowed back and forth across a several-block area. The Central Security conscripts made no serious attempts to advance on the crowds, focusing instead on holding their ground and letting the tear gas do the work for them. Protesters repeatedly scattered and regrouped, relentlessly attacking the police lines with their bare hands (the rocks would come later) and displaying a ferocity that was only matched by their level of organization. Makeshift triage units sprung up—nothing fancy, just water, vinegar, and onions for those overcome by the gas.

There were new tear-gas treatments on display. At one point, as I emerged gagging and spluttering into a side street, a man splashed some Pepsi onto my burning eyes; it immediately alleviated the pain, and by the end of the day I was carrying a cola bottle and helping other people. (Numerous protest organizers and participants have since told me that this innovative cola treatment was a direct import from the experiences of the Tunisian revolutionaries.) Volunteers distributed vinegar-soaked surgical masks to anyone who didn't have one. Those on the front lines attacked in loose shifts, with organizers in the crowd encouraging those who had taken a brief rest to return to the clashes so that others could step away.

Wael Khalil fought in the battle of Galaa Bridge, and credits the efforts of what he calls the "unknown soldiers of the revolution." A line of ambulances and paramedics had set up shop alongside the Giza Sheraton and spent hours retrieving and treating those who had been injured or overcome by massive and prolonged tear-gas exposure. Khalil, at one point, was near collapse and he recalls a paramedic basically dragging him to safety and administering an oxygen mask.

With the beginnings of the gas bombardment, the crowd's mood turned from triumphant to livid. Tempers began to fray, targeted not just at the police but at other protesters and innocent bystanders. On a side street just outside of the battle zone, there was a near fistfight over just how violently to fight back. A young man in his twenties was having a meltdown and being held back by others, who amazingly (a little naïvely, actually, given what was already happening) pleaded with him to maintain a nonviolent stance. The young man screamed back "Peaceful? Are you serious! After this?"

I managed to approach the enraged man; he identified himself only as "an Egyptian citizen" and bluntly told me, "I expect the government to fall today. There will be dead bodies in the streets. I have nothing to lose anymore. I have a degree in information technology, and I've been sitting at home for the past three years."

Just over the young man's shoulder, a near riot was taking place outside an upscale supermarket. The terrified manager had attempted to lock the front door to prevent protesters from seeking refuge. Several people went ballistic and seemed prepared to shatter the market's glass doors. Moderately cooler heads prevailed, and after a tense negotiation, the manager, probably saving his store, agreed to pass out a huge sack of onions and several bottles of vinegar. Others along the same street were offering assistance without being threatened. One woman dropped a bag of onions from her third-floor window to the grateful protesters below.

Bizarrely, this same stretch of side street leading toward Galaa Bridge also had a string of five packed troop carriers from Central Security, parked and waiting in reserve—which meant the riot police on the bridge were also teargassing their own colleagues. Inside the trucks, miserable Central Security conscripts sat, desperately tying shirts around their eyes and pouring water on their heads to endure the lungfuls of gas they were inhaling. To make their day complete, they were also basically surrounded by enraged protesters. Amazingly, nobody attacked the trucks, even though they were heavily outnumbered and deep into what could definitely be considered enemy territory. The worst thing they were subjected to was a steady stream of verbal abuse. I watched one man in his thirties screaming at the soldiers, "They're sitting in their offices giving orders and you're out here setting the streets on fire!" A soldier with streaming red eyes displayed what seemed to be genuine anguish and replied, "What can we do? It's in spite of ourselves."

It was a revealing exchange; one variation of which was seen at several different protests. It also went a long way toward explaining the curious relationship between Egyptian protestors and the frontline troops in charge of repressing them. Among longtime activists, there has always been a general acknowledgement that the Central Security troops were some of the biggest victims in the whole equation. Generally stocked by illiterate rural conscripts, Central Security was the regime's cannon fodder, occupying the lowest and least respected rungs of the Ministry of Interior ladder. Even when they were beating on you, it was hard to hate them; they always looked underfed, undereducated, and bullied by their own officers. Back in 2004–2005, when the Kefaya protest movement was flowering, one of their more novel tactics was to directly appeal to the Central Security guys, engaging them in conversation, handing them bottles of water and devising chants that expressed sympathy for their plight. One such slogan was dusted off and reintroduced by the chanting crowds on the twenty-eighth: "Oh unfortunate soldier/tell us how much they pay you!"

All of which explains why, in the aftermath of the revolution, there was never any vengeance or animosity directly at Central Security—nothing like the visceral hatred reserved for the elite and powerful State Security Investigations agency. On January 28, the crowds weren't violently attacking Central Security because they were hated; they were violently attacking Central Security because it was necessary in order to break the back of the police state so the real revolution could begin.

Several participants in the January 28 protests vividly recall moments of genuine empathy with their Central Security adversaries. At one point, relatively early in the day, Hisham Kassem was one of several hundred people waging a back-and-forth struggle on the October 6 Bridge. A comparative lull in the hostilities was suddenly threatened by the advance of a fresh contingent of Central Security forces coming aggressively up a ramp that leads past the (at that point, still intact) National Democratic Party headquarters. Kassem was appointed elder statesman of his group and sent forward to negotiate with the officer in charge and hopefully prevent a fresh round of violence. "He told me, 'I swear, sir, these are my orders. It's not my choice. I'll get in trouble if I retreat.' He was terrified," Kassem said.

Later on and to the south, Ahmad Abdalla and another group of protesters found themselves penned in place by a thick wall of Central Security lines on a side street leading to the mouth of the Kasr al-Nil Bridge. Just a few meters away a fierce battle was raging halfway across the bridge, but Abdalla and his friends couldn't get through the lines to join the fray. For more than an hour, the protesters and the soldiers imprisoning them were stuck in place a few feet apart and enveloped by tear gas.

"You start to make a kind of relationship with them. We would give them water and cigarettes. They were suffering from the gas as bad as anyone so we would give them vinegar-soaked tissues," Abdalla said. "We felt like they were all trapped there together."

This inherent empathy between the two warring sides would become crucial later on in the evening, when the power dynamics dramatically shifted and hundreds of Central Security cadres found themselves outnumbered and at the mercy of the protestors.

As the battle for Galaa Bridge continued to ebb and flow, I surveyed the scene and conducted interviews; once again I was struck by the sheer diversity of the crowds, and by how many female protesters were there. One fifteen-minute stretch of consecutive interviews conducted on the same intersection underscores the kind of cross section that turned out that day to call for the end of the Mubarak era.

Rabab Al Mahdy, a westernized young woman who teaches political science at the American University in Cairo, told me, "This is an authoritarian regime so protests are an expected reaction. What's unexpected today is the number of people." A few minutes later, a plump middle-aged veiled woman shouted at me, "We don't have an agenda, we only want the fall of the regime and all its symbols. We're not the Muslim Brotherhood and not the Wafd Party. We're all against oppression and corruption. This is a failed regime."

Next to her stood Nadia Hassan, another middle-aged *muhaggaba* (veiled woman) with a long history of political activity—she was a longtime member of the Nasserist Party and the Egyptian Organization for Human Rights. Hassan told me, "We don't just want the fall of

Mubarak. We want the fall of the whole regime. This regime is worried and this violence is the proof, shutting down the communications is the proof. They're scared of us, and they should be." Hassan Yassin, a thirty-one-year-old executive at a multinational corporation (he declined to name the company) was standing next to her. Seemingly educated and well-off (he was filming scenes on his BlackBerry), Yassin nonetheless sounded as angry and fed up as anybody. "I'm drowning in my own country," he told me. "Why should I be afraid of a police officer that I pay taxes for?"

Yassin said that before he left his home that morning, he told his young daughter, "I'm doing this for you." Now he was out among the rock throwers expressing complete contempt and distrust for basically every player in the game, other than the protesting masses.

"They're all dogs, every single one. I don't trust any of them—not the government, not the opposition parties, not the Americans, and not ElBaradei."

Finally I met an impoverished young man named Mido. He was twenty-three and looked younger; he'd had to drop out of college because his family couldn't afford to have him not working. Now he made LE300 (about $55 per month) working in a grocery and routinely had to watch the area's senior police officers swagger through the store and grab merchandise for free.

"If this government continues, this city and this country will become hell," Mido said. "Now I'm supposed to enter the army. Can you imagine me in the army serving this government?"

Mido paused for second and summed up with a little lyricism, concluding, "The youth in this country have stopped even dreaming."

At about four in the afternoon, the phalanx of Central Security troops broke ranks and ran, leaving their paddy wagons behind. For a while it was hard to even grasp what had happened. Protesters gleefully spray-painted slogans on the trucks—some of which still contained terrified Central Security guys.

It was a powerful moment—the exact turning point when the police realized the people weren't afraid of them and that they were badly outnumbered. There was a surreal interlude while the protesters casually flowed around the remaining pockets of disoriented police on the bridge. A few shell-shocked Central Security troops remained behind, taking shelter inside their trucks. At least one paddy wagon driver was hopelessly and tearfully pleading with protesters not to trash his truck, saying he would be punished if anything happened to it. (They left him alone but totaled the truck.)

Interior Ministry officers gathered impotently on the small bridge, while the protesters merely ignored them and surged past. I walked past one group of officers huddling around a walkie-talkie and heard one of them say, "Nobody's answering." In an instant, the fearsome and hated bullies of the Interior Ministry had become pathetic and irrelevant. One middle-aged officer carrying a baton still hadn't figured it out. He started yelling at a group of young protesters photographing the remains of the paddy wagons. One passing demonstrator simply stuck a finger in the officer's face and loudly shushed him. The officer stopped for a moment, thought it over, and meekly withdrew.

Back in Galaa Square, a spirited debate ensued over what to do next. Many of the protesters were determined to continue to Kasr al-Nil Bridge and push on to Tahrir. Others argued to stay put for strategic reasons, holding onto the square so that security reinforcements couldn't close ranks behind them. One older man shouted, "It's better if we control multiple places than just gather in Tahrir where they can bottle us up." Another responded, "If we stop moving, people will start to go home."

On Kasr al-Nil Bridge, the final gateway to Tahrir Square, the scene was far more violent and chaotic. The clashes at Galaa Square were tame by comparison; here there was genuine bloodlust in the air. Police had been pushed halfway across the bridge but were responding with indiscriminate use of tear gas and rubber bullets. Protestors were now responding with barrages of rocks.

As with the Galaa conflict, the protesters worked in organized shifts; those returning from the front lines of the conflict were treated for tear-gas exposure and buckshot wounds by makeshift triage units while others surged to the front to continue the conflict. Protesters dragged a blanket loaded with hundreds of rocks and concrete chunks toward the front to be thrown at the police. One man yelled, "Keep up the pressure. Two more hours of this and they'll collapse!"

Even approaching the front lines halfway across the bridge was difficult. Rocks were raining down on both

sides, and young men holding bloody wounds were staggering back for treatment. On the narrow confines of the
bridge, the tear-gas barrages proved less effective; brave
young protesters would merely flip the canister a few
feet over the side into the Nile, which foamed with nox-
ious bubbles. But the officers had also begun employing
buckshot. I watched a young man bleeding from multiple, small pellet wounds in his face being carried limply
off the bridge and into a car.

Abdalla, who had spent more than an hour trapped on
a side street near the conflict zone, eventually managed
to make it onto the bridge. "I saw one of my best friends
get shot right in the face with buckshot. He had thirty-
eight pellets in his face, two of them in his eye," he said.

The amount of tear gas in the air was crippling; Salem
and his dedicated team of tear-gas catchers were on the
scene, but having a hard time keeping up. "Three or four
tear-gas canisters every fucking second. It was relent-
less," Salem said.

In addition to the barrages coming from the bridge
itself, Central Security gas squads had also set up position on the grounds of the Cairo Sporting Club, enabling
them to attack the protesters' right-hand flank before
they could even get near the bridge. Salem also insists he
saw two teams of police officers firing tear-gas barrages
from a pair of boats floating on the Nile.

After a while, Salem's gas mask—which was designed
to block paint fumes and simply not built for this kind of
workload—started to malfunction. He gagged, vomited,
and nearly passed out at the entrance to the Cairo Opera

House. When he had recovered a bit, he adopted a new role. Salem is a big guy—about six feet three inches tall and thickly built—so he spent an hour or so dragging the injured away from the front lines. Eventually, as exhaustion set in, he retreated northward into the inhabited section of Zamalek Island and took shelter in a prearranged safe house.

Just after 4:00 P.M., an enormous volley of tear gas and rubber bullets drove the crowd off the bridge and north into Zamalek in the direction of the Cairo Tower, the Gezira Club and the venerable Marriott Hotel. The security forces pressed their advantage, moving forward behind further gas barrages and setting off a panicked scramble for safety. Wael Khalil was among those repulsed from the bridge in that charge; he and a group of several dozen hard-core protestors began searching for an alternative way to the river. They attempted to cross the May 15 Bridge, which runs right past the Marriott, but security was amassed there as well and they were beaten back again.

It was then that Khalil witnessed an unexpected moment of revolutionary comedy. A bus filled with foreign tourists emerged from the Marriott and attempted to cross the bridge to the Tahrir side, right into the teeth of the conflict. What the tourists on board were thinking was anybody's guess, but the Egyptian bus driver was apparently having the time of his life. Khalil made eye contact with the driver, who smiled broadly and mo-

tioned for the protesters to get behind his bus and use the vehicle as a shield as he drove through the police lines. This strategically dubious plan didn't get far; the Central Security guys simply let the bus move slowly through and closed ranks behind it. Eventually expelled from the May 15 Bridge as well, Khalil ended up crossing all the way back to the Giza Governorate side of the river. There he received a glimpse of just how widespread the day's rebellion had become. To the north of the bridge, he could clearly see a vicious battle raging—complete with Molotov cocktails and burning tires—in the Nile-side district of Kit Kat.

I was also on Kasr al-Nil Bridge, when the police made their devastating 4:00 P.M. charge and temporarily routed the protesters. A several-hundred-strong group of angry beleaguered young people retreated, making its way by side roads and across the Opera House grounds back to Galaa Square to rest and regroup. Just as the defeated Kasr al-Nil veterans were straggling back to the square, around 5:00 P.M., something amazing happened. About three thousand protestors were still holding on to the square. Suddenly a huge crowd of marchers appeared from the direction of Giza in the south. They looked to be at least five thousand strong, and their arrival set off a huge roar. One of them told me they had come from Giza Square (where Mohammed ElBaradei had received his first-ever whiff of tear gas) and had been fighting their own running battles all day before finally breaking through the security lines.

Their arrival was a massive morale boost, a new cry was started up of "To Tahrir!" One protestor, witnessing the scene, said, "It's over, finished. This is the beginning of the end for Mubarak."

Tarek Shalaby, a twenty-seven-year-old IT professional, recalls the moment when this second wave surged onto the scene and headed for the front lines. He had spent hours at Kasr al-Nil and was nearing collapse. "I was sitting on the sidewalk, completely exhausted and gassed out, and all of a sudden there were thousands of fresh reinforcements," he said. "It was like, 'Yes! This is exactly what we need.' One of the guys put his hand on my friend's shoulder and said, 'Just rest. We'll take over.' It was perfect."

At that point, I had to leave to start filing my first batch of stories in time for a *Times* of London deadline. Without Internet or cell phone service, I had to improvise. So I walked back to the BBC offices fifteen minutes away in Agouza where I knew they had a functioning satellite Internet connection, and basically bartered computer access for as much television and radio punditry as they needed.

It was from there that I managed to catch up on what the rest of the country had been enduring. Outside the capital, Alexandria and Suez had witnessed similar upheaval, with Central Security defeated in both places. Suez was an absolute war zone, with protesters violently taking control of parts of the city and torching dozens of

police stations. The residents of Egypt's major Suez Canal cities—Suez, Ismailia, and Port Saieed—have long been known for their toughness, fiercely resisting separate occupations by the British and Israelis, and the residents of Suez upheld that reputation.

Alexandria, where Khaled Saieed was a hometown martyr, was equally fearsome—and an even more dramatic rout took place there. According to multiple eyewitnesses and participants, the Battle of Alexandria on January 28 was angrier, more destructive, and much shorter than its Cairo counterpart. In Cairo, Central Security was fighting hard in several locations until just before sunset. In Alexandria, police and Central Security disappeared from the streets several hours earlier.

"They managed to exhaust the security forces early on," said Rawya Rageh, the Jazeera International correspondent who covered the events in Alexandria that day. "It was obvious from three P.M. on that the police were losing."

The differences between Alexandria and Cairo on January 28 seemed to stem from equal parts geographic realities and localized psychology. It's safe to say that by 2011, the police were despised all across Egypt, but in Alexandria the hatred was particularly fresh and visceral. In addition to the lingering animosity from the Khaled Saieed case, Alexandrians on January 28 were dealing with an entirely new "emergency law martyr" case.

On New Year's Eve 2011, a bomber struck outside a large Coptic Orthodox Church in Alexandria during midnight mass, killing twenty-three and injuring dozens more. It was an embarrassment for the Interior Ministry—proof that the security and stability it claimed to provide under the emergency laws were a mirage.

In the wake of the bombing, police unleashed a massive crackdown on the city's thriving community of Salafists—Islamic fundamentalists who are far more conservative than the Muslim Brotherhood. It's unclear whether there was ever any hard evidence to connect the city's Salafists to the church bombing, but circumstantially the community had been stirring up religious tensions in Alexandria for months, regularly conducting angry demonstrations outside of local churches—including the church that was attacked in the New Year's Eve bombing.

This wave of anti-Christian protests was spurred by the case of Camellia Shehata, a young Coptic mother who disappeared from her home in July 2010. The wife of a Coptic priest, Shehata's disappearance was originally treated as a kidnapping. But within a week she was found living safely with a friend in Cairo and returned by authorities to her home. From there, the Egyptian rumor mill started to grind. According to the version embraced by the Salafists and many other Egyptian Muslims, Shehata had in fact converted to Islam in order to escape an abusive marriage. Authorities, the rumors stated, dreading the headache of a public conversion controversy involving a priest's wife, returned her against her will to her husband and the church—which locked Shehata up in a monastery in order to brainwash her back to Christianity.

Whatever the truth, the issue was embraced by Salafists as a pretext to launch a wave of antichurch protests.

Badly Photoshopped pictures of Shehata wearing an enveloping conservative Islamic veil circulated widely. A subsequent video statement by Shehata herself, calmly denying any such conversion and emphasizing her Christian faith, was dismissed as proof she was being coerced into obedience.

All of which explains why police in Alexandria chose to target the city's Salafist communities after the New Year's Eve bombing. Hundreds of young Salafist men were rounded up for questioning—a routine enough occurrence in Mubarak's Egypt, especially after a major terrorist attack. But what made this case unique was the absolute veil of silence thrown over it by the government—which refused to release even the barest details of who had been arrested or what, if any, charges they faced. Local human rights organizations complained that the families of those arrested were being threatened by police to prevent them from talking to the media or seeking outside help.

The crackdown quickly produced its first martyr. Sayed Bilal, a thirty-one-year-old welder and Salafist, was arrested on January 5. The next day, family members said they were summoned to a local hospital where they found Bilal dead and his body bearing signs of torture. The family initially filed an official complaint and spoke to journalists about their case. But then they reversed course and refused to speak to or cooperate with local human rights organizations. Several human rights workers reported that Bilal's brother had been arrested after Bilal's death and that Bilal's family was warned that they would never see him again if they continued to speak out. A delegation from the Nedim Center tried to visit the Bilal family home, but were prevented by police officers from even approaching the building.

Sobhi Saleh, an Alexandria lawyer and former Muslim Brotherhood parliamentarian who lost his seat in the notorious elections two months earlier, expressed utter mystification at the government's tactics. Such behavior, he said, was outside the bounds of even the Emergency Law—which already gave the state wide-ranging powers of indefinite detention.

"It's like we've been occupied by a foreign power. Alexandria has become an occupied country. I feel like we need to appeal to the United Nations Security Council," Saleh told me, three weeks before the revolution. "This is beyond even the Emergency Law. Can you imagine? We've reached the point where you say, 'I wish they were applying the Emergency Law.'"

The church bombing case was never solved, and Sayed Bilal most likely enters the history books as the final pre-revolutionary casualty of the Mubarak regime.

In addition to the nastier-than-usual relationship between Alexandria's police and its citizens, security forces in the coastal city faced a very different strategic challenge from that faced by their counterparts in the capital. Cairo is a city of bridges, all of which serve as natural choke points where Central Security could gather and effectively halt the protesters' movement. The bridges neutralized the protesters' superior numbers, hindered their ability to surround the riot police, and enhanced the effectiveness of the Interior Ministry's weaponry. That's why many of the most violent and iconic battles on January 28 took place on bridges. But Alexandria, which sprawls along the Mediterranean coast, contains very few such natural bottlenecks; it was a logistical nightmare.

It's possible that police commanders in Alexandria were completely aware of that strategic disadvantage, and also that they knew quite well just how badly they were despised by the local population. That would explain their decision to strike hard and fast from the very start of the day—teargassing worshippers at the Qaed Ibrahim Mosque before they could even start protesting.

Whatever the reasoning, it didn't matter in the end. On January 28, the police in Alexandria didn't stand a chance—immediately finding themselves surrounded, overwhelmed, and dealing with multiple fronts. Within a few hours of chaotic running battles, the Interior Ministry's presence on the city's streets had melted away, and the crowds were focused on their long-awaited vengeance.

"By four P.M., you couldn't find a police officer. By six P.M. there was hardly a police station left standing," said Haitham Mesbah, Khaled Saieed's close friend. "The people were determined to destroy every police station in the city."

Zeyad Salem, a twenty-nine-year-old dentist and English teacher, recalls watching a police station in the Bab Sharqy district being overrun by an enraged mob. Inside the station, he witnessed a senior officer in a black sweater tear the epaulets off his shoulders, toss them aside, and desperately attempt to escape by blending in with the crowd. "People were furious," Salem told me. "There were a lot of people who had been arrested and tortured and they knew specific officers and were coming for them."

With the police surrendering comparatively early, Alexandrians had plenty of extra time to seek out and destroy symbols of the regime. For a while, it became open season on anything Mubarak. In Ramle Station Square, a seaside public space that's one of the natural hearts of downtown Alexandria, one of the first targets was a mysterious set of green posters hanging from dozens of downtown streetlamps and openly advocating Gamal Mubarak as Egypt's next president. The posters had suddenly appeared several months earlier, shortly before the November 2010 parliamentary elections. It was the most blatant public indication yet of Gamal's presidential ambitions. But locals had no idea who had ordered or financed the campaign and Gamal's camp professed innocence. On January 28, one of the first things the protesters did was shimmy up the light poles and tear down every single Gamal Mubarak poster.

Haitham Mesbah recalls marching with several thousand protesters past a twelve-story apartment building in the Laurent district that had a huge poster of Hosni Mubarak erected on the roof. The doors downstairs had been padlocked by frightened residents, but the demonstrators convinced them to open it. Several young people headed up to the roof to tear down the offending picture as the crowd below roared with approval.

It wasn't just the youth who were expressing their

frustration and rage that day. Salem recalls seeing three elderly women marching together—all of them seemingly in their seventies and walking with canes. "One of them put her hand on my shoulder and asked me to walk her up to a huge poster of Mubarak hanging in front of the local NDP office," Salem said. "Then she reached up and hit it twice with her cane. She didn't do any damage, of course. She had no strength. But she just needed to do it."

Back in Cairo, Central Security held out until just before sunset—making a pair of dramatic stands on the Kasr al-Nil and October 6 bridges. The two structures are roughly a half mile apart, and the combatants on one bridge could clearly see what was happening on the other. Over on the October 6 Bridge, Kassem had spent much of his day moving back and forth along the same stretch of asphalt as the battle ebbed and flowed. By 5:00 P.M., he estimated that the crowds on the bridge had swelled to about ten thousand. The tide was turning and a day of violence had stoked the young protesters into escalating bloodlust.

"The kids started stopping cars passing by and siphoning the fuel into water bottles," he said. "That's when I decided it was time for me to leave."

Just before sunset, the police lines on Kasr al-Nil finally broke ranks in the face of fresh pressure from the thousands of newly arrived protesters. Abdalla crossed the bridge and witnessed the scene of the Central Security transport being overwhelmed by enraged youth in front of the Nile Hilton.

Down the Corniche, the demonstrators turned their attention to the suddenly unprotected National Democratic Party headquarters building—site of Safwat al-Sherif's memorable proclamation of Egypt's stability less than thirty hours earlier. The war was far from over; pitched battles were still raging just up the Corniche outside the Ministry of Information building. A particularly vicious conflict was still taking place on Kasr al-Aini Street—the southern entrance to Tahrir Square where police were using live ammunition and sniper fire to defend the streets leading to the Parliament Building and the Ministry of Interior itself.

But despite the violence still taking place around them, many protesters couldn't pass up the opportunity to ransack the NDP building. It was like a well-earned victory cigar at the end of an extremely hard day. Abdalla watched as several young protesters scaled the fence around the building's interior garden and unlocked the gates from the inside. The free-for-all was officially on. This wasn't really regarded by the participants as looting; after all, stealing from the people who had stolen from your country for generations was practically patriotic.

One man emerged from the building carrying a massive plasma television set, and sold it on the spot for LE500—about $85 dollars. Another had managed to secure a set of plush leather desk accessories—blotter, agenda, letter opener, pen cup, etc. Laying his wares on the ground, he called out like a street vendor: "Ten pounds for anything, ten pounds for anything."

Some people were refusing to buy in on principle, saying, "I don't want anything from the National Democratic Party." But others clearly saw this as an opportunity for a bit of radical revolutionary redistribution. One such protester emerged from the building with an armful of ice-cold sodas liberated from an NDP refrigerator. Abdalla gratefully accepted an apple-flavored Fanta. At this point fires started in multiple locations by looters were already starting to spread.

By the time Mohamed El Dahshan appeared on the scene, the NDP headquarters was already in flames—but protesters and looters were still streaming in and out of the smoldering building. Several cars parked in the courtyard were burning as well, and some protesters were trying to pry open the trunks *while* the cars were on fire.

"There were families, a guy, wife, and child pushing leather desk chairs into the street. Some guy had found a box of Qurans inside and was handing them out free to people," El Dahshan told me. "I saw a guy coming out with three cartons of milk. Really, it was anything they could carry away."

Feeling conflicted by what he was witnessing, Abdalla climbed a set a stairs onto the October 6 Overpass—a several-miles-long structure that connects to the bridge of the same name and runs directly behind the NDP building and the Egyptian Museum. With a bird's-eye view of a city in convulsions, he paused to reflect.

"I don't smoke, but I borrowed a cigarette from a friend. I lit it and opened my apple Fanta and watched the NDP burn for a while," he said. "People were congratulating each other but I felt a little scared, actually. I love downtown Cairo and it was painful to see scenes of destruction."

With the NDP building officially a lost cause, concern began to grow among the protesters about the safety and security of the Egyptian Museum. The low-slung red-domed building houses a treasure trove of Egypt's rich archeological history—much of it badly maintained and chaotically archived. There was little hope that a fire truck would appear on the scene, so the demonstrators could only hope that the flames from the NDP building wouldn't spread across the communal wall shared by the two structures. The demonstrators turned their attention to making sure the museum wasn't looted during the chaos. People here had vivid memories of the widespread looting that plagued Baghdad after Saddam Hussein was defeated. Some looters had already broken in; *Times* of London reporter James Hider witnessed as a squad of volunteers entered the building, dragged out several aspiring thieves, and aggressively strip-searched them. A second group of volunteers, some of them carrying riot batons, formed a human chain around the building. One of them passionately told Mohamed El Dahshan, "Cairo is not going to be another Baghdad."

At one point, the volunteers spotted someone hiding in the shadows on the museum grounds. They scaled the fence and dragged the man out, but he turned out to be a terrified straggler from the Tourism Police whose job in normal times was also to protect the museum. Caught by surprise by the fall of Tahrir, he had been hiding out for fear that the protesters would attack him as a symbol of the government.

About an hour later, when the army appeared on the scene, they moved quickly to secure and search the museum. Abdalla watched as one of the soldiers aggressively interrogated another young man who had been found hiding inside.

"The soldier was ordering him to empty his pockets and the kid was claiming to be one of the volunteers, saying, 'I was trying to protect the museum,'" Abdalla said. "The soldier pulled a handful of silver bracelets out of the kid's pocket and immediately slapped him hard across the face."

As expected, a curfew was announced, and was immediately defied not only by the people in Tahrir but by thousands of citizens who took to the streets after hearing the news that Tahrir was in the hands of the demonstrators. News broke that Mubarak had ordered the deployment of the army in the city center for the first time in decades—a final sign that the Interior Ministry had been conclusively defeated.

The massive October 6 Bridge was surreally quiet; a little light traffic was flowing but there wasn't a single uniformed officer in sight. Even the roadside kiosks of the traffic cops were empty. A steady stream of people came from the direction of Tahrir, many carrying a motley array of goods obviously looted from the NDP building. Citizens walked past carrying printers, leather office chairs, and other office equipment—plus a variety of riot shields and batons. One pedestrian told a man carrying an office chair, "Shame on you." He responded, "No, it's okay, it's from the party."

The NDP headquarters was still actively burning; it would continue smoldering for days and gawkers gathered on the bridge to take pictures of it. The army was already on the scene in Tahrir. After years of observing the increasingly toxic relationship between the Egyptian people and the country's police forces, I had no idea what to expect once I reached Tahrir. What I found there was entirely surprising. The tanks and armored troop carriers were indeed out in force, clustered in the square and parked in front of the burning shell of the NDP headquarters.

And the protestors? They were happily scrambling up onto the vehicles to pose for cell phone pictures and chatting casually with the tank drivers. I watched as one extremely patient tank commander made the universal sign for "wrap it up" to a couple of young protestors conducting an extended photo session.

It was a much tenser scene down the Corniche at the Ministry of Information, where another contingent of soldiers was fending off a crowd of about eight hundred hard-core protestors trying to invade the building that also houses all of the state television and radio stations. The crowd was desperate to get in, but I watched a senior army officer stand in the center of the scrum and conduct a remarkably calm debate with the protestors. It ended with a mutual embrace between the officer and the most prominent protest leaders—an exchange that would be basically unthinkable with any senior police officer.

Asking different protestors about their views on the army, the responses were fairly uniform. One young man said, "There's always been respect between the people and the army. They are the protectors of the people and today they're helping to protect us from the police."

Another, more blunt, perspective: "The army soldiers are all right. The police are sons of bitches!'"

But not all of the protestors shared that same automatic trust for the army. That first night in Tahrir, there was already a healthy share of animosity on display. As one tank moved into position outside the Egyptian Museum, a man shouted, "We should welcome them. They stopped the violence."

Another responded, "Welcome them? We should beat them!"

Protestors had openly berated and shoved soldiers—who once again showed impressive patience. The actions of a few protestors toward the soldiers were so aggressive that one could only conclude the soldiers were under direct orders not to retaliate.

Abdalla, the young movie director, recalled the moment when the tanks arrived in Tahrir. "The people said from the start 'The army is here, the army is here' and they ran toward them like they were guardian angels."

That night, Hosni Mubarak made his first public statement to a nation newly in revolt against his government. It was a strange performance. Mubarak seemed drained and a little disconnected from the moment, mainly keeping his eyes on the speech in front of him on the podium and rarely making sustained eye contact with the camera. Mubarak, in interviews, had tended to be a very plain-spoken man displaying an earthy charm that probably appealed to many of his citizens. But here he seemed to hide behind flowery political rhetoric that only added to the overall sense of detachment.

Mubarak started his speech by essentially blaming everything on the protesters, saying the day had started as a legitimate exercise in peaceful freedom of expression, but had been corrupted by shadowy unnamed "infiltrators" and transformed into "chaos and riots" that threatened the fabric of the nation. He expressed deep regret at "the loss of innocent lives among the citizens and the police forces," and actually credited the police forces for the restraint they showed before apparently being provoked into a fight by aggressive protesters.

"There is a fine line between freedom and chaos and while I favor the people's freedom to express their opinions, I must also maintain Egypt's security and stability," he warned.

Mubarak referred frequently to what he considered widespread "chaos and mayhem," that have "left the majority of Egyptian people fearing for Egypt and its future"—seemingly ignoring the fact that all of the destruction so far had been directed solely against the Interior Ministry forces and his own ruling party. In conclusion, Mubarak announced that he was dissolving the cabinet and would be appointing a new prime minister in the coming days.

In Tahrir, about ten minutes after the speech ended,

the reaction was not the one Mubarak might have hoped for. The protesters, after a violent and bloody day, scoffed at this latest concession. It didn't even anger them—it was too ridiculous. As one man said, laughing, "Have you heard anyone this week shouting, 'Down, down with the cabinet'?!"

The message was received loud and clear, and Mubarak still didn't get it: The problem was him.

10

Thug Rule

A holding pattern ensued as a nervous nation struggled to come to grips with its post–January 28 reality. It had been a dizzying couple of days. On the twenty-fifth, Egyptians had broken through the emotional and psychological barriers of fear, helplessness, and apathy that had kept them oppressed for decades. On the twenty-eighth, they had broken through the physical barriers of the police state. But what would happen now?

The Tahrir protesters were basking in their victory and entrenching for the long haul—bringing in blankets, tents, and food. The police had completely vanished, but there were already encouraging signs of self-governance on display in the community.

On the morning of the twenty-ninth in Giza, several of the main intersections were already staffed by volunteer residents helping to keep the traffic moving. Egyptians, for years, had engaged in a laundry list of negative behaviors, from high-level corruption to things as simple as rampant littering, sexual harassment, and significantly, acting like selfish jerks in traffic. Now they were starting to feel like the country was theirs again, and taking personal responsibility for its condition.

Ominously, there was a mysterious series of breakouts at several prisons around the capital—fueling concerns that a vengeful Ministry of Interior had thrown open the jailhouse gates and was seeking to plunge the nation into chaos until the ungrateful citizens begged the police to return and restore security.

Mobile phone service returned on the twenty-ninth, but the Internet would remain shut down for several more days. Strangely, one obscure Internet service provider named Noor remained operational. The company held just a tiny sliver of the home Internet service market. But it provided Internet and communications services for several vital economic cornerstones, including the Cairo and Alexandria Stock Exchange, the National Bank of Egypt, and a handful of large multinational corporations—a possible reason why the government had decided to leave it alone.

In a wonderful coincidence, Noor also provided the in-house Internet service for two Cairo hotels—one of them being the Intercontinental, which directly overlooks Tahrir Square. As word of this unexpected loophole spread, journalists (myself included) began flocking to the hotel, setting up shop and taking up residence.

———

The concessions from Mubarak continued. On the twenty-ninth, it was announced that Omar Suleiman, longtime head of national intelligence, had been named as vice president—the first-ever vice president of the Mubarak era. This was a curious bit of strategy by Mubarak. Suleiman was certainly well known to Egyptians; for years he had been considered a potential dark-horse candidate to succeed Mubarak as president. But most people really had no idea who he was, beyond the barest biographical details.

For years, Suleiman had been seemingly everywhere and involved in everything, either at Mubarak's side offering counsel or shuttling between Jerusalem and Washington, D.C., for high-level talks. He was the ultimate consigliere—nobody ever heard him speak publicly and he never gave speeches or interviews. For all his name-recognition value, he might as well have been the Wizard of Oz. The closest anyone got to hearing what Suleiman actually had to say was in some of the Wikileaks cables—where he railed against the national security threats posed by Hizbullah and Hamas and seemed nearly obsessed with the looming threat posed by Tehran, at one point offering an American diplomat the use of existing Egyptian spy networks in Iran.

Among the protesters, Suleiman's appointment was widely (but not universally) rejected. He was regarded by the majority as essentially an extension of Mubarak and his regime. And the fact that he was liked and trusted in both Washington, D.C., and Jerusalem didn't exactly bolster his reputation either. At one point, in the middle of revolutionary Tahrir, two men were seen passionately debating Suleiman's merits. One seemed to be trying to talk himself into Suleiman as a viable transitional leader of a post-Mubarak government, saying, "He's a good man, and he has a lot of international experience."

The caustic response from his companion: "Are you kidding me? Omar Suleiman is the dirtiest man in Egypt. Just look at who his friends are!"

The return of the mobile phone networks turned out to be a bit of a mixed blessing. Suddenly Egyptians could pick up the phone again and start terrifying each other by swapping rumors of the widespread chaos, looting, and lawlessness engulfing the city. The disappearance of the police and the news of the prison breaks didn't help. State television, which was actively pushing the chaos angle, made things even worse. As night approached, many citizens seemed to sincerely believe that bands of criminals and convicts were raping and pillaging their way across the city like a marauding Viking horde.

There was definitely an element of class-based hysteria fueling things. Middle- and upper-class Egyptians seemed convinced that Cairo's millions of slum dwellers were about to rise up en masse and recreate Bastille Day. There was a sense that many Egyptians didn't trust themselves (and definitely didn't trust their fellow citizens) to behave themselves in the absence of police authority.

In retrospect there certainly was some looting that

night. In Mohandessin, an upscale neighborhood of Giza, several stores on Shehab Street and a large duty-free outlet store on Arab League Street were ransacked. Elsewhere, a string of businesses on Pyramid Street—home to a concentration of sleazy nightclubs and cabarets—was gutted, as was the Arcadia Mall to the north of Tahrir and a branch of the international department store chain Carrefour. But it was never anywhere near as bad as people thought at the time—or as bad as it might have been in a different city. (Try suddenly removing every single police officer in New York, Los Angeles, or Paris and watch what happens.)

This free-flowing anxiety produced yet another example of the citizens taking responsibility for vanished authority. All across the city, neighborhood watch groups sprung up to protect their districts. In Agouza, shortly after sunset, a neighborhood militia set up a barricade on the Corniche below the building where I was working. I spent an hour chatting with the volunteer guardians, finding them a motley bunch, with an eclectic array of weaponry. In addition to the usual assortment of sticks and clubs, there was an impressive collection of knives, swords, machetes, and the occasional homemade spear. One man was brandishing a weight-lifting bar; another had somehow gotten his hands on a field hockey stick.[3]

The volunteers were fired up by rumor-fueled fear and

---

3 In more than a decade of living in Egypt, I have never heard of anyone playing field hockey. Karate, yoga, rugby, and even synchronized swimming, yes, but to this day I still have no idea where you would even go to buy a field hockey stick.

by a passion to protect their homes. They also seemed just a little too twitchy and primed for a fight. Several reported horrible tales they had heard about bands of marauding thieves laying siege to different neighborhoods. But nobody had actually witnessed anything. Still it was hard to fault their obvious pride and sense of community—something Egypt had sorely lacked in recent years. As one of the militia leaders told me, "We don't need Mubarak. We don't need the army or police to protect us. This is the Egyptian people."

Anytime someone new approached, on foot and especially in a vehicle of any kind, the alarm whistles would sound and the volunteers noisily gather to confront the interloper. ID cards would be checked and a several questions asked; if you weren't from that neighborhood, you needed to have a really good reason to be out and about that night.

There was the sense that anybody who was judged not to look right or even anyone who displayed the slightest bit of attitude during the questioning would be arbitrarily denied passage and possibly beaten down on the spot.

Many of the Tahrir protesters retreated to their home neighborhoods on the night of the twenty-ninth to participate in the volunteer protection groups. IT professional and protestor Tarek Shalaby spent an evening at the barricades in Mohandessin, but concluded that his fellow neighborhood watch volunteers were "hysterical and really classist." He didn't come back after that first night, spending most of the next two weeks living full time in Tahrir.

"Sandmonkey" Salem spent several nights serving on the front lines of his neighborhood militia in Heliopolis. "I was actually having a ball," he laughs, recalling nights brandishing a baseball bat at a checkpoint and helping his fellow volunteers make Molotov cocktails. "They were some of the greatest nights of my life."

One experience in particular sticks in Salem's mind from that chaotic post–January 28 period—conclusive proof that at least some of the claims to "chaos and looting" were in fact part of a cynical plan to sow fear by a defeated and embittered Interior Ministry. From the start, one of the most persistent rumors was that the police and State Security officers were playing an active role in the criminality—either looting businesses themselves or simply driving around and firing into the air to give the impression that the city was slipping out of control without them. One of the reasons so many of the neighborhood militias were checking IDs was to make sure the newcomer wasn't an Interior Ministry employee.

One night, Salem heard the alert whistles ring out and saw his neighborhood militia attacking a pickup truck that had tried to run the barricade. Inside the truck he found four men carrying machine pistols and police IDs. The interlopers were enthusiastically roughed up and imprisoned in a local mosque, eventually being turned over to the military.

"Let's be clear on something: this wasn't looting. This was police officers practicing terrorism," Salem said.

Later that night on the twenty-ninth, I had a chance to explore the neighborhood militia phenomenon from up close. At about two in the morning, I left the BBC offices and headed home to Giza—a long walk but a straight shot southward along all major thoroughfares. Not sure what to expect out there, I stuck exclusively to wide and well-lit streets. The city was almost completely empty of vehicle traffic. It was a chilly night and many of the volunteer checkpoints had fires burning to provide warmth.

At one of the first checkpoints I crossed, I was surprised to find a trademark blue police pickup truck and an actual police officer in uniform, complete with pistol on his hip, chatting casually with the militia guys. There appeared to be at least one police station that was not only intact and partially staffed, but was actively assisting the residents in protecting their district. It was a nice and necessary reminder that not every man who wore that uniform was a villainous power-mad bully. Certainly the internal culture of the police forces had long ago gone rotten, and there seemed to be no mechanism or oversight—inside or outside the Interior Ministry—to prevent a bad officer from basically doing whatever he wanted. But there were also officers who joined the force for the right reasons and retained the sense of mission and public duty that defines a proper police force. That night, especially given the context of the preceding days, it was good to see an officer who took his duties seriously, and equally gratifying to see that the residents weren't blinded by hatred of the Interior Ministry and could recognize that this officer was one of the good ones.

I walked for more than an hour that night, running

into a new group of neighborhood watchdogs every few intersections. Each time I would present my ID and tell them where I was going. In every case, I was treated with warmth and respect. But I also easily passed whatever visual profiling standards they were applying—I wasn't poor and wasn't fresh out of jail.

Others weren't so fortunate. At a checkpoint near the Galaa Bridge (site of one of the pivotal battles the day before) I watched as a man in a grubby *gallabeya* gown was roughly detained by the local neighborhood watch group. The man's hands were tied behind his back, and he was being aggressively shoved along as he tearfully professed innocence and pleaded to be released. I asked several different people just what the man had done to earn this treatment, and received several different answers. As far as I could tell, his crime was being impoverished and living across the city with no plausible reason for being in that neighborhood that late at night. It seemed entirely likely that this was a variation on the old American urban cliché: Instead of driving-while-black, he was guilty of walking-while-poor.

I relaxed and moved on toward home, once the group announced it would turn this alleged marauder over to the nearest army checkpoint. At least then I knew that the man wasn't going to be subjected to some sort of spontaneous frontier justice.

In the following days, both protesters and the military moved to reinforce their positions in Tahrir. The army continued a steady buildup of forces, moving tanks across many of the entrances to the square and starting to check ID cards of those seeking to enter. There was a sense of fragile cooperation on display—far from actual trust, but many of the civilians seemed desperate to prevent any fraying of relations with the military.

At a checkpoint line at the entrance to Tahrir, some of the protesters bristled at the new security procedures. One civilian immediately climbed on a tank and shouted, "Cooperate with the army! The army and the people are together today. But we must be careful because there are people who want to come here and turn us against each other."

Each day brought several new military truckloads of waist-high concrete barriers that were unloaded and assembled around the perimeter. It was as though they were trying to physically cut Tahrir Square off from the rest of Egypt.

Despite the appeals for cooperation and the emergence of a fresh chant—"The people and the army are one hand!"—there were already signs of how quickly that harmony could deteriorate. At one point on January 30, hundreds of protestors—apparently alarmed by the steadily increasing army presence—physically blocked a pair of fresh tanks from entering the square.

Some of the protesters were also making their own aggressive moves, repeatedly attempting to overrun the Ministry of Interior itself, which is located about ten minutes southeast of Tahrir. Vicious battles raged for two days in the surrounding streets, with the remnants of the police and special forces using live ammunition and sniper fire to defend their citadel. According to multiple witnesses and participants, army soldiers on the scene generally stood by and watched as civilian demonstrators were gunned down.

Figuring out just where the military stood in all this became everyone's favorite guessing game. So far they had been gentle and almost sympathetic with the protesters, but nobody had any illusions but that the military had been one of the biggest beneficiaries of the Mubarak era—and the two military regimes that had preceded him. Inside Tahrir, whether or not you trusted the army's intentions became the litmus test as to how optimistic you were about the future. One young protester—an engineer in his mid-twenties who declined to give me his name—said his single biggest concern going forward was, "The army. I hope that they won't take a U-turn. I don't think they will but it's something to worry about."

Mubarak, meanwhile, seemed to understand that his armed forces—more than any other national institution—had so far retained the respect of the people. In addition to Suleiman's elevation to vice president, Minister of Civil Aviation Ahmed Shafiq (like Mubarak, a former air force commander) was announced as the new prime minister. By stacking his new governmental team with distinguished military figures, Mubarak seemed to be hoping that their respect and reputation could paper over his own endangered legitimacy.

At about four in the afternoon on January 30, there

came a potentially disturbing development. Just as the latest curfew was coming into effect, a pair of military jet fighters flew over Tahrir, fast and low, several times, rattling windows and jarring people's nerves. It was reminiscent of the Israeli psychological warfare tactics displayed in the Gaza Strip. If the jets had flown slower and at a higher altitude, the crowd would have probably seen it as a show of solidarity. But the eardrum rattling nature of the flyovers could only have been an intimidation move. It fueled speculation among the protestors that the soldiers were preparing to drop their previously tolerant attitude and turn their weapons on the crowds.

The next morning's *Al-Ahram* newspaper seemed to confirm everyone's worst fears. A red banner headline in the January 31 edition of the state-owned flagship daily proclaimed, "Mubarak meets with his military commanders." The accompanying photo showed Mubarak and Suleiman deep in conversation with the military's chief of staff General Sami Enan.

Despite the concerns about just what was being discussed behind closed doors between Mubarak and his generals, protesters continued to press the advantage—feeling that time and momentum were on their side. A call was issued for Egypt's first-ever "Millioneya" or million-man gathering in Tahrir on Tuesday February 1, marking the one-week anniversary of the revolution. This would be the first true test of the protesters' larger pool of support across Egypt, a window into whether or not they could really claim to represent the desires of the Egyptian people. The government responded by shutting down all railroad service to Cairo, presumably to prevent a mass influx into the capital from the provinces.

Late in the evening on January 31 there came a pivotal turning point, one that seemingly kicked the revolution into a new gear. The military issued a brief statement acknowledging "the legitimacy of the people's demands" and guaranteeing that all peaceful freedom of expression would be protected. The statement made a point of noting that all acts of looting or criminality would be harshly suppressed and concluded with a crucial sentence: "Your Armed Forces have not and will not resort to the use of force against this great people."

This last element was a huge relief to the Tahrir protesters. You could actually feel the mounting public tension dissipating. There was still a healthy contingent among the protesters that would never trust the soldiers under any circumstances, but they were a definite minority at this point. The army's statement was regarded by many as the first public sign that Mubarak and his military were not on the same page. Some protesters cited the earlier meeting between the president and his generals and connected the dots—concluding (without any proof of course) that the army's statement was, in fact, a response to the Mubarak meeting. In the minds of the most optimistic protesters, the military had just received their Tiananmen orders and refused to carry them out.

One smaller development from this time frame that would dramatically mushroom in importance later on in the revolution: by January 30 and 31, things had calmed down enough that the protesters could take stock and do a bit of a head count. It was then that word began to spread on Twitter and through the media that Wael Ghonim, a young Egyptian who worked in Dubai as a marketing executive for Google, hadn't been seen since January 28.

Tuesday's Millioneya was a dramatic success. Tahrir is an absolutely huge public space, and for most of February 1, it was too packed to even move around comfortably. From up above, it was even more impressive; you could hardly find a patch of unoccupied asphalt. Multiple stages had been set up by now, and the atmosphere was equal parts angry rally and jubilant street party. From every direction came defiant speeches, clever new chants, and infectious bursts of music or drumming. There seemed to be about one hundred separate rallies happening at once, all melding into one unified revolutionary organism.

Mubarak's anchors of support appeared to be visibly crumbling before everyone's eyes. U.S. officials started to toss around phrases about the "need for an orderly transition"—wording that most protesters took to mean that Washington was willing to see Mubarak put to pasture, but wanted to retain the same basic structure and relationship: Mubarakism as usual, just without Mubarak.

Prominent officials and celebrities started breaking with the regime and publicly speaking out. A delegation of senior judges came to Tahrir together, carrying a banner

that read: "The people and the judges are one hand." In an interview with the BBC, no less an Egyptian icon than Omar Sharif backed the protests and called for Mubarak's departure. "I think Mr. Mubarak is very stubborn about not leaving. He doesn't want to be humiliated," Sharif said. "I think most Egyptian people, if they're going to vote, will vote against Mr. Mubarak, I am sure. They want new people and they want a real democracy, which is wonderful because they had never thought of democracy before. I had never heard anyone in Egypt speak of democracy."

ElBaradei, who had visited Tahrir a day earlier and was nearly stampeded by well-wishers, was back at home and giving merciless interviews. Mubarak, he said, had no choice but to step down.

"We are already discussing the post-Mubarak era," he told the Arabeya satellite news channel. "There can be dialogue but it has to come after the demands of the people are met and the first of those is that President Mubarak leaves."

Among the protesters, there seemed to be a growing belief that Mubarak's reign was entering its final hours. People simply couldn't envision how he could hold out much longer after this.

"He's going, that much is sure. After all this, there's no way he can stay. We're not scared anymore, he's going," Ossama Zaki, the forty-five-year-old owner of a small paint production company, said as he waited on line to enter Tahrir. "I hope he leaves today, God willing. But tomorrow is okay too."

They would all, of course, be disappointed—at least

for the moment. That evening Mubarak made his second address to the nation, and poured a dose of cold reality on anyone who thought he would give up this easily. It was a performance worthy of extended study. Mubarak remained defiant but came off as a little wounded (like a father dealing with unappreciative and resentful children) and basically admitted that he had lost control of the situation. As with his previous speech, he started by blaming the protesters—once again emphasizing that whatever was happening in Tahrir was a perversion of legitimate freedom of speech that was being "mobilized and controlled by political forces that want to escalate and worsen the situation."

The protests, he repeated nearly verbatim from his first speech, "began with noble youths and citizens practicing their rights to peaceful demonstrations, expressing their concerns and aspirations. But they were quickly exploited by those who sought to spread chaos and violence."

Mubarak in this second address sounds far more engaged and self-assured, particularly compared to his January 28 speech when he seemed a little shell-shocked, taken aback by the day's events. This time, he sounds very much like a man running for public office and seeking to make a personal connection with the viewers.

"I direct my speech today directly to the Egyptian people—Muslims and Christians, old and young, peasants and workers, and all Egyptian men and women in the countryside and cities and in all the governorates.

I have never, ever sought power and the people know the difficult circumstances in which I shouldered my responsibility and what I offered this country in war and peace, just as [the people know] I am a man from the armed forces and it is not in my nature to betray the trust or abandon my responsibilities and duties."

With the pleasantries and self-congratulations out of the way, Mubarak gets down to the part everyone was truly waiting for. "I say in all honesty and regardless of the current situation that I did not intend to nominate myself for a new presidential term. I have spent enough years of my life in the service of Egypt and its people. I am now absolutely determined to finish my work for the nation . . . I will work in the remaining months of my term to take the steps to ensure a peaceful transfer of power."

In conclusion, he, oddly, starts speaking of himself in the third person, talking in terms of his legacy.

"Hosni Mubarak, who speaks to you today, is proud of the long years he spent in the service of Egypt and its people. This dear nation is my country, it is the country of all Egyptians, here I have lived and fought for its sake and I defended its land, its sovereignty and interests. On this land I will die and history will judge me."

So there it was: Mubarak would be leaving power, but on his terms. The rest of his regime would remain intact. He would take the next six months as a sort of extended victory tour, then head off into the dictatorial sunset—content in the knowledge of a life lived well and in the service of his nation. And by the way, he had always intended to do this, so nobody could say he was forced out.

Not surprisingly, this latest concession was immediately rejected in Tahrir, where Mubarak's speech was projected live onto a giant improvised screen. The anti-Mubarak chants, and more than a few thrown shoes, started as soon as he had signed off. At this point, hard casualty numbers from the past week were starting to come into clearer focus, and the protesters were not in a forgiving mood. They also had no intention of granting Mubarak a leisurely six-month victory lap, then continuing forward living under the exact same NDP police state. With each new half-concession, the protesters seemed to get more motivated, and more pissed off.

"It's a political game. He's buying time," Khaled Maghrabi, an executive at a drug company, commented in Tahrir, shortly after the speech. "After the death of three hundred martyrs this week, I can't accept having him for one minute more."

But Mubarak's speech wasn't aimed at protesters like Maghrabi. His message was carefully calibrated to resonate in the Egypt that existed outside of Tahrir Square. Mubarak had shifted strategies and was now playing a long game—entrenching and stretching out the standoff, keeping the country disrupted while blaming the protestors for that disruption. If he couldn't crush them or placate them, he would isolate and outlast them.

It was a valid strategy. Many apolitical Egyptians were already showing signs of revolutionary fatigue at the massive interruption of daily life. The Internet was still blocked, banks and the stock market were closed, the trains to Cairo weren't running, most work had been suspended, and stores in some areas were running low on supplies. This latest concession offered the tantalizing prospect of a rapid return to normality.

There was also a deeply personal element to Mubarak's February 1 appeal to his people, one that did resonate with many ordinary Egyptians and robbed the protestors of at least some of their popular support. Mubarak actually *was* viewed as a genuine war hero and father figure by many Egyptians, who often forgave his faults and blamed his underlings for systemic problems like corruption and police brutality. Even those who were happy to see him go didn't necessarily see the need to have him humiliated along the way. He could also count on his still-formidable media machine to paint him as a beloved father figure whose efforts were unappreciated and who had earned the right to at least leave the stage with dignity.

In retrospect, this turned out to be step one of the government's counteroffensive. That night saw the beginning of the second, much nastier, step: the rise of the first pro-Mubarak rallies.

the moment. Still there are only so many times you can fend off a direct request from your editors, so there we were.

In the opposite lane, coming from the direction of the Pyramids, we spotted what looked like a one-thousand-person march of pro-Mubarak supporters chanting slogans like "We love the president" and "He's not going."

Some of the protesters were riding horses and camels—apparently tourist workers coming from the stables clustered around the Pyramids. At the time, my colleagues and I thought it made for a great journalistic visual. Hours later, those same horses and camels would be used in a bizarre, medieval mounted charge into the unarmed civilians occupying Tahrir.

Just after noon, we were returning on that same stretch of Pyramid Street (having failed to secure our interview) when Internet service abruptly returned. Finally able to access Twitter from my phone for the first time in more than a week, I quickly learned that the pro-Mubarak demonstration, which first seemed like a harmless diversion, had become something much darker. Thousands of pro-Mubarak forces had gathered in Abdel Moneim Riyadh Square, just to the north of the Egyptian Museum, and were moving aggressively toward Tahrir.

"We could see them coming from Abdel Moneim Riyadh. People quickly moved to secure the square near the museum," said Mohamed El Dahshan. "Things were still civil at this point, [there was] just shouting."

Mohab Wahby claimed he knew in advance that there would be trouble that day. In the morning his uncle, who lived in Maadi, called to warn him that he had seen mini-vans full of guys coming out of the home of the local NDP parliament member.

As the two sides grew closer, there was a strange calm-before-the-storm period as both assembled within feet of each other in front of the museum, yelling conflicting slogans.

"There were maybe forty centimeters between them," El Dahshan recalled. "That lasted maybe ten minutes. It was too explosive to stay nonviolent."

The army soldiers, meanwhile, who had been diligently checking IDs and banning anyone carrying a weapon just an hour earlier, suddenly withdrew from the scene. Those who remained simply stood on their tanks and watched the developing hostilities. At 1:40 P.M., Sandmonkey tweeted: "[A] 1000 pro-Mubarak demonstration is heading towards Tahrir. The military is withdrawing. This will get ugly quick."

The confrontation soon developed into rock throwing. The pro-Mubarak protesters unleashed a massive charge, pushing so deeply into the square that they overran a stage being set up and smashed all the audio equipment. A second front opened up as another group of armed men attempted to penetrate Tahrir from the direction of Talaat Harb Street. The situation inside Tahrir became fearful and desperate. The protesters in the square had been taken by surprise, and they scrambled to recover and organize their defenses. Mohamed El Dahshan recalls an initial period of panic and disorganization.

"You had people running and you had no idea where they were running to or from," he said.

They simply were not prepared for this; the previous days had been a bit of a lull, and many in the square had allowed themselves to relax a bit. Some of the hard-cores had gone home to grab a hot shower and sleep in their own beds for a night. The numbers in Tahrir had thinned out. When those who were still in the square realized that the army wasn't going to protect them, there was a moment of despair for some.

Tarek Shalaby recalls spotting two army soldiers on a nearby rooftop passively filming the whole confrontation.

"I had a bit of [a] nervous breakdown . . . I was crying and screaming at the same time. I couldn't believe they were just filming us killing each other," he said. "I thought it was over—that if we lose this, the revolution has failed."

Sherine Tadros, a correspondent for Al Jazeera International, rushed to Tahrir as the clashes began and actually found herself trapped outside of Tahrir and surrounded by the pro-Mubarak forces.

"They all constantly asked me my loyalty," Tadros recalled. "I got asked so many times. 'Are you with us or not? Are you with Mubarak?' I'd say 'I'm with the president, of course!'"

At one point, Tadros was caught up in a mini-stampede and ended up pinned against a green wrought-iron fence surrounding a nearby sidewalk. Several men from among the pro-Mubarak forces started to aggressively grope her body in the middle of the clashes. As she hunched over to protect herself against multiple sets of invasive hands, another pro-Mubarak protester came to her rescue—fending off her attackers and physically tossing her to safety on the other side of the fence.

By the time I made it back to Tahrir at about two in the afternoon, the scene there couldn't have been more different from the euphoria of the preceding days. The protesters in the square were being besieged from multiple directions, and I saw dozens of bloodied young men staggering or being carried away from the front lines.

Tahrir is a huge public space with at least nine major entry points, and the pro-Mubarak crowds continued to probe the edges, seeking a soft way in. In addition to the museum entrance, two other intersections were active conflict zones. At the entrance to Kasr al-Nil Street, stones and bricks thrown by pro-Mubarak forces started landing more than fifty meters from the front lines. Protest leaders on microphones organized the defenses, summoning teams of youths to different intersections. Shalaby vividly recalls a man on the loudspeaker yelling, "Listen, people! We won't be able to pray right now. We're in a state of war. So never mind the prayers now, and God will accept it. Right now we need fifty more people at the museum and one hundred at Talaat Harb . . ."

A middle-aged man walked past with blood streaming from the back of his head; a veiled woman held his arm and guided his steps and she kept hysterically repeating, "We won't die. God is with us. We won't die."

The mood among the protesters was paranoid and enraged. They were convinced that their attackers were largely made up of plainclothes officers from the police and State Security—basically the revenge-seeking remnants of the police state that had skulked away the previous week. They were determined not to break ranks and to remain vigilant against the threat of infiltration by provocateurs. With the soldiers abandoning their duties, the protesters started organizing their own inspection procedures at the square's entrances. Everyone approaching Tahrir was repeatedly frisked and forced to show their national ID card—which would show on the back if the holder was employed by the Interior Ministry or was a member of the NDP.

One man was apparently unmasked as an Interior Ministry employee; and the crowd nearly killed him before others dragged them off and sent the bloodied man off to a makeshift prison that had been created in an underground subway station. One protest leader with a megaphone was reading off the full names and personal information from ID cards taken from alleged plainclothes security officers. Mohamed El Dahshan posted a picture on Twitter of a dozen confiscated police IDs.

At about three in the afternoon there came a moment that will live forever in the YouTube Hall of Fame: the Tahrir Horse and Camel Charge. In Egypt, the events of February 2 are now almost universally referred to as "the Battle of the Camel"—a reference to an actual historic battle from the early days of Islam. But one of the underreported aspects of this chaotic day is that the mounted charge, while making for great television, was strategically meaningless and a tactical disaster. The riders managed to penetrate deep into the square, but they basically outran their own ground support and quickly found themselves surrounded in enemy territory. A few of them managed to ride back to safety, but the rest were dragged from their saddles by enraged protesters and savagely beaten.

"I saw two of those guys covered in blood. I'm pretty sure one of them died," said Shalaby, who said that the Tahrir protesters immediately drew confidence from the incident and launched their own countercharge.

Throughout the day, the army's behavior was, at the very least, puzzling and potentially very suspicious. The soldiers sitting on their tanks seemed to be passively observing the battle despite desperate pleas from the Tahrir protesters.

"It wasn't just that they weren't doing anything. They were complicit. They let these guys through," El Dahshan said.

At one point, El Dahshan asked an army colonel on the scene, "Why aren't you doing anything?" The officer replied, "Aren't you expressing your opinion? They're here expressing their opinion as well."

A lower-level soldier told El Dahshan, "We're only stopping people from entering with weapons."

El Dahshan replied, "But they have bricks, man!" The soldier waved him off and turned his back.

One man seized the microphone and issued an angry call to the army forces. "Make a decision now," and defend the peaceful protesters, he shouted. But as his criticisms of the military grew more strident, others wrested the microphone from his hand. One youth yelled at him, "We don't want to turn the people against the army!"

At 5:00 P.M., as I left the square to begin writing, it seemed depressingly certain that the Tahrir protestors were in a losing battle. They were undermanned and already running short on bandages, antiseptic, and painkillers to treat the steadily mounting number of casualties. Already the calls were going out on Twitter for emergency reinforcements and supplies. But if the pro-Mubarak crowds succeeded in surrounding Tahrir and blocking all the entrances, these reinforcements would have no way of reaching their besieged colleagues.

As a spectator, I felt certain that if the Tahrir protesters could hold out until Friday, then vast numbers would flock to their cause. But their chances of holding out that long looked slim. They were going to be slaughtered. As I left, a middle-aged man saw my notebook and asked frantically, "Are people coming? Do you know? Are the youth coming to help us?"

It's indicative of the mood of the day that Wahby can't help but speak of it in medieval terms, saying, "It was just hordes of people attacking you, and you're stuck there defending the castle."

The two groups charged and countercharged, amid jarring changes in momentum. At one point, Tarek Shalaby overran his group and the momentum shifted. In a scene that would have been comical in any other context, he went from chasing the pro-Mubarak supporters to turning and running with a mob at his heels. He tripped, sprawling on the pavement, thinking he was about to be beaten to death, but a stranger hauled him back to his feet.

"I never saw that guy again," Shalaby said. "It was just a few seconds, but he saved my life."

As sunset approached, the Tahrir protesters improbably seemed to gather strength and organize more sophisticated defenses. Dozens of blue squares of sheet metal, part of the fences surrounding a pair of construction sites, were cannibalized and turned into makeshift barricades. Spotters developed the tactic of banging stones against streetlights to send out the alert of an impending attack and summon reinforcements.

"After five or six at night, the war drums started," said Shalaby, who fought on the front lines until dawn.

The clanging of the streetlight alarms was joined by another sound—the constant rhythmic pounding of concrete being broken down into chunks by metal bars. Wahby still keeps an audio file on his phone of the hypnotic sound of the projectile factory in progress (the file is named "The sound of freedom").

The action at the other intersections died down and

the wide corridor between Tahrir and Abdel Moneim Riyadh Square became the primary front. The quarter-mile
stretch of pavement directly in front of the Egyptian
Museum became no-man's-land.

"They would throw ten rocks, and we would throw one
thousand and keep throwing. It was like carpet bombing,"
said Wael Khalil.

At the front lines, particularly daring volunteers would
stand on cars and act as spotters—braving the hail of
stones and shouting out the locations of the pro-Mubarak
forces. Shalaby spent much of his time at the front blindly
lobbing his rocks like mortar shells wherever the spotters were pointing.

"I could have killed three people, or I could have
thrown all my stones harmlessly into no-man's-land. I
have no idea," he said.

A sort of improvised military assembly line developed
inside Tahrir to equip and arm those heading toward
the front. First there was what Shalaby called "the
shield station" where people would wrap your head and
chest in protective layers of cardboard. After that was a
huge pile of rocks and concrete chunks for throwing. A
different set of volunteers focused exclusively on breaking up concrete to replenish this armory. Others made
forays to the front lines with armfuls of fresh rocks, as
well as water and *halawa* (a sweet local candy made
from sesame seeds) to keep the fighters' energy up. At
one point, Shalaby was taking shelter behind one of the
metal sheets as rocks from the pro-Mubarak side rained
around him. "Suddenly there were two young girls next

to me right at the front lines, passing out water bottles to the fighters," he said. "It was amazing. These girls had balls of steel!"

Ahmad Abdalla, the young movie director, made one brief disastrous foray into the front lines, but was quickly pointed to a more supporting role.

"I started throwing rocks and it became obvious that I was terrible at it. I was afraid I would hit some of our own people," Abdalla said, laughing. "Other guys noticed as well and told me, 'Don't throw, go break up concrete for more rocks.'"

During this frantic defense of Tahrir, the presence of the Muslim Brotherhood and other Islamist groups appears to have played a crucial role. While Shalaby insists that he didn't notice a greater concentration of Brothers along the front lines than any other group, other participants credit the Brotherhood cadres with helping to organize the defenses, devise spontaneous frontline strategies, and turn the tide.

"If it wasn't for the Brotherhood, we would have gotten really screwed that day," El Dahshan recalled. "They went to the front lines. Their people really shouldered a lot of the burden on defense."

Mohab Wahby adds, "It was the Islamists who came up with the whole damn strategy . . . That was the first time I realized the extent of the Islamist presence."

The pro-Mubarak forces developed more advanced techniques as well. As evening fell, they started climbing up to the roofs of buildings across the street from the museum and punishing the Tahrir protesters with rocks,

Molotovs, and even bottles of acid. Sherine Tadros, the Jazeera correspondent, had taken shelter at this point in the home of a family that lived just outside of the conflict zone. She spent a sleepless night on a balcony reporting her observations live on television over a mobile phone. At one point, she witnessed a pro-Mubarak Molotov cocktail factory in action in a nearby intersection. A man sat in the middle of the street with a huge plastic container full of gasoline, methodically filling a succession of soda bottles. Every few minutes a woman would approach with a crate of empty bottles for him to fill and then carry off a dozen freshly created firebombs to be hurled at the Tahrir protesters.

Shalaby still bears permanent scars on both his hands from being splashed with a mysterious liquid that burned his skin and ate huge holes in his pants. He says the only reason he wasn't more seriously wounded was due to the long underwear he had on to ward off the winter chill. With drops of acid scarring his hands and face, he retreated into Tahrir and stopped by the overwhelmed medical clinic.

"Of course there were hundreds of people being treated, so the doctors didn't have time for anyone who had anything less than an open chest wound," he said. "The doctors took one look and told me to put some water on it."

The pro-Mubarak protesters' move to higher ground gave them a massive strategic advantage that lasted several hours. Shalaby recalls at least fifteen people stationed on one particular roof; from that vantage point and distance they were able to launch devastating attacks with lethal accuracy. The Molotov cocktails, while dramatic, did comparatively little damage since the protesters could see them coming and scatter. It was the high-speed rock barrages from above that caused far more serious casualties.

"A good portion of our deaths came from the people on that building. Rocks were coming down on us from the fifteenth floor and we had no way to reach them," Shalaby said.

It took more than three hours, until past 10:00 P.M., for the Tahrir protesters to overcome this strategic disadvantage. Using the blue sheet metal from the construction site as a sort of turtle-shell armor, they inched forward slowly toward the entrance of the building in question—which was deep into no-man's-land.

"Once we started to get near the entrance of the building, that's when they had to run," Shalaby said. "They knew if we were able to reach the door and get up to the roof, they would have all been killed."

The taking of that crucial high ground proved to be one of the turning points in the battle for Tahrir. By 11:00 P.M., the pro-Mubarak forces on the ground had largely melted away, and the Tahrir protesters enjoyed a brief lull. Shalaby and Wahby both said they were so exhausted at that point that they fell asleep for a while, sitting on the concrete.

At about two in the morning, an even more violent and deadly attack kicked off. The protesters, by now, had extended their perimeter to the back end of the Egyptian

Museum in the shadow of the October 6 flyover. Suddenly there came a fresh hail of rocks and Molotov cocktails from up on the bridge itself. Shalaby said he saw about fifty men on the bridge using slings to launch the projectiles; they wore civilian clothing, but he insists they must have been police officers.

"You can tell an officer by the way he stands," Shalaby said.

Even worse, this new attack was backed by at least one sniper, according to multiple participants. Nobody ever actually saw this shooter, only the deadly effects of his work.

"I would hear three or four gunshots, and then see three bodies being pulled back right then and there," Shalaby said. "It was immediate."

The protesters, having already vanquished the first wave of attacks were undaunted, demonstrating incredible bravery and literally laughing in the face of death.

"A kid fell right in front of us and the others carried him away," said Mohab Wahby. But every time the sniper claimed a new victim, other protesters would literally rush into the kill zone and dance mockingly.

"It was a 'Fuck you!' Like they were saying 'Yeah, give us more,'" Wahby said.

This fresh standoff lasted several more hours, with the Tahrir protesters taking heavy casualties and unable to even reach their attackers. Wahby described the mood among the frontline fighters at this point as one of pure murderous rage—a willingness to kill any of their assailants they could lay their hands on.

"It was like, 'These aren't humans, they're animals not worthy of mercy. They're trying to kill us for LE50,'" he said.

Finally, at about two in the morning, a group of protesters managed to infiltrate through the darkness under the bridge, climb one of the entrance ramps, and outflank the attackers on the bridge with a sustained barrage of rocks. The fighters on the ground used this distraction to advance as well. Just as the remaining pro-Mubarak forces were about to be surrounded and probably slaughtered, the military mysteriously chose that moment to intervene for the first time that day.

"That's when the army got involved and started firing in the air to separate the two sides," said Shalaby, who said whatever fragile trust he had in the military died that day. "They could have done that ten hours earlier, but they decided to move just as we were about to win."

It took more than twelve hours of nearly continuous fighting, and cost the lives of at least twenty-six protesters plus hundreds of serious injuries, but the Battle of Tahrir had been won.

"In retrospect, I feel like we were never really in any true danger. These people were not going to succeed in running us off the square," said Wael Khalil. "But at the time, yes we were scared."

The following day, Thursday, February 3, witnessed no serious attacks on Tahrir Square. But the remaining pro-Mubarak mobs re-emerged and moved to choke off Tahrir's supply lines, controlling bridges and other access points.

It was the journalists' turn to feel the terror of mob violence. All through the day came steadily increasing reports of journalists—both foreigners and native Egyptians—being harassed, detained, and even assaulted by pro-Mubarak crowds or arrested by the army.

I had my own serious scare with an angry mob, far away from Tahrir Square in the middle-class district of Dokki. Once again I was with Hider and Garcia-Navarro, plus Merrit Kennedy, a young American living in Cairo who had been drafted in mid-revolution onto the National Public Radio team. We spotted a street-side cart serving *fuul* (the national dish of cooked fava beans) and decided this was a fine chance to chat with ordinary Egyptians about the difficulties and uncertainties of the past ten days. We stopped by, introduced ourselves, and started, with me playing translator, to ask a few innocuous questions about food supplies and daily life. Were the stores reopening? Were people returning to work?

The situation turned bad almost immediately. Garcia-Navarro's oversized microphone was an attention magnet, and after perhaps four questions, hotheads in the crowd that had gathered began demanding to see our identification and expressing suspicion of our intentions. I'm still not sure if they thought we were spies or if just being journalists was bad enough. One man asked aggressively if we were "from that Jazeera channel that we're all so disgusted by." I responded, in retrospect, perhaps a little too sarcastically, asking if he saw any television cameras with us.

Suddenly one man started swinging at me, and half of

the crowd immediately turned into a mob. I was struck in the face at least four times. Garcia-Navarro, a veteran war correspondent and no stranger to violence, cleverly faked a fit of weeping hysteria, which seemed to get the guys to back off a bit. After about a minute of scuffling, cooler heads in the crowd managed to pull me to relative safety and told me to get out and make for our waiting taxi. As I was speed-walking away, someone came up and touched my shoulder; I wheeled around ready for another fight, but it was only a young man bringing me my slightly mangled eyeglasses, which had been abandoned at the scene.

I arrived at where our taxi was parked up the block only to find an entirely new standoff in progress. Hider, Kennedy, and Garcia-Navarro had made it into the taxi but were now penned in by another angry mob. They were banging on the windows and trying to get inside. One man parked his motorcycle directly in front of the car to block any escape.

As the only Egyptian in the group, I became the focal point for the mob's anger. My accented Arabic (I was raised in the United States) only heightened their suspicions. One man kept yelling in my face, "You're not really Egyptian. Who exactly are you?" I managed to produce my Egyptian passport and my driver Gamal started pleading with the crowd, telling them that he had known me for ten years and knew most of my family.

The Egyptian passport did more harm than good—largely because it states clearly that I was born in America. With the paranoia and xenophobia on display, that was more than enough to make me a target. In a moment of dark comedy, the crowd started shouting to turn us over to the police or the army. I responded, "Yes, please! Find me a soldier. I'll turn myself over. I need somebody to save me from *you*!"

I was beginning to genuinely fear for our safety, savoring the bitter irony that after more than a decade in Cairo, I was about to be beaten to death in the street about five minutes away from where one of my aunts lives. Thankfully an officer from the military police appeared on the scene from a nearby checkpoint, and immediately helped bring some calm to the situation. Against the protests of the crowd, the officer managed to get me into the taxi, and in order to keep us safe, escorted us to a walled-in courtyard. There we found another group of terrified journalists—this time all native Egyptians working for a local English-language paper. They too had been rescued from an angry mob by the army. Clearly, similar scenes were playing out all across Cairo.

In fairness, I can't classify my own personal experience as part of some coordinated campaign by pro-government forces to harass journalists. Our attackers were just ordinary Egyptian citizens whose nerves had been frayed by ten days of uncertainty and unrest. State television fueled their anxiety with a steady diet of conspiracy theories claiming that shadowy foreign influences were behind the waves of civil unrest and that foreign journalists were hopelessly biased in favor of the anti-Mubarak protesters—thus actively helping to bring the regime down.

But elsewhere something far more systematic and sinister seemed to be taking place. The list of incidents is long.

The Cairo Bureau Chief of *The Washington Post,* Leila Fadel, and several reporters from Al Jazeera International were among more than a dozen journalists detained for hours by the army. Others were treated far more roughly by mobs of enraged citizens. A Greek journalist was stabbed in the leg; Andrew Lee Butters, a reporter working with *Time* magazine, was detained and roughed up by civilians, whom he saw taking orders from uniformed police officers on the scene.

CNN's Anderson Cooper, along with a producer and cameraman, was attacked by crowds, who punched them and attempted to break their camera; his CNN colleague Hala Gorani was also attacked. ABC's Christiane Amanpour was chased away from a street interview in progress. When she and her crew returned to their car, they were surrounded by men who banged on the sides and broke the windshield with a rock. They escaped without injury. A Reuters television crew was attacked while filming in the streets outside of Tahrir. The offices of the Arabeya satellite news channel were overrun by an angry mob, leaving one reporter hospitalized.

"They are now targeting anybody with a camera, notepad, anybody interviewing people—anyone will get violently attacked, anyone they could get their hands on," warned Mohamed Abdel Dayem, the North Africa coordinator for the Committee to Protect Journalists. "If you're a journalist in Egypt at this late stage in the game, they don't care if you're from Mars—they're going to come after you."

It wasn't just the journalists getting mobbed that day either. Anyone who seemingly sympathized with the Tahrir Square protesters was targeted—often with the active support and participation of the remnants of the police forces.

Mahmoud "Sandmonkey" Salem was attempting to reach Tahrir on the morning of February 3 with several friends and a carload of food and medical supplies. He headed for the Talaat Harb Street entrance, hearing from friends that it was secure. But several blocks away from the square, he found his car surrounded by a mob screaming, "Who are you with? Who are you with?"

Salem tried to drive through the crowds to safety but found himself blocked. He found a cluster of men wearing police uniforms up the street and desperately turned to them for help, only to see them join in with the mob. "The police were encouraging the people to come and attack us," Salem said.

The police and the mob searched the trunk of his car and found the supplies they were carrying. One of them shouted, "Oh you're here to help the saboteurs!"

Another searched the wallets and purses of Salem's companions and found a five-dollar bill—which really set the crowd off. "They were waving the five dollars in the air and shouting, 'Here's the money they've taken from the Americans and the Jews,'" Salem recalled.

At one point, Salem emerged from the vehicle to appeal for reason. He was punched in the face several times and sought shelter back inside as the crowd attempted to tear the car apart with them inside. "The police were jumping up and down on the hood and other people were tearing off the side mirrors," he said. "It was like a zombie attack movie."

Eventually the army intervened and everybody was hustled off to a nearby police station, where they were held for several hours and then released. That day was a turning point for Salem. Until then, his identity as the popular blogger Sandmonkey was known only to his circle of friends. When he emerged from police custody, he went home, called CNN, and outed himself to the world while angrily describing the day's experiences.

Later that night, Mohamed El Dahshan had his own mob experience. While trying to get home, he ran afoul of a civilian checkpoint. When they searched his bags and found a laptop computer, he was immediately attacked.

"That's all they needed to see. The laptop meant I was a Facebook person, which meant I was a foreign agent," he said. "They pretty much dragged me out of the taxi, beat me up for a little while, and turned me over to a nearby army officer."

The sheer scope of the number of violent incidents in one day immediately discredited any government argument that these were isolated or spontaneous events. The U.S.

State Department, in a serious escalation of its prior rhetoric, angrily dismissed that possibility from the start.

"I don't think these are random events," said State Department Spokesman P. J. Crowley. "There appears to be an effort to disrupt the abilities of journalists to cover events."

In a bit of surreal irony, many of these attacks took place at the same time that new Prime Minister Ahmed Shafiq was apologizing for the previous day's violence and promising an investigation. This two-day spasm of violence backfired badly on the Mubarak regime, rallying both domestic and international support for the Tahrir protesters and their cause.

"There were a lot of people who were against the revolution until that day, and came out and joined," said Tarek Shalaby, who said he personally knew several people who became enthusiastically pro-revolution after February 2.

Attitudes seemed to harden among the foreign journalists as well. Anderson Cooper, in particular, emerged from his Egyptian ordeal as a fierce anti-Mubarak campaigner with a massive public platform. Upon his return to the United States, Cooper went on a memorable tear, harshly criticizing the Mubarak regime at every opportunity. On February 9, he appeared on *The Late Show with David Letterman* and flatly described Mubarak as "the dictator of Egypt for thirty years and finally his people have had enough and they're trying to get basic rights."

In describing his attackers, Cooper told Letterman,

"They were basically thugs. Whether they were hired directly by businessmen aligned with Mubarak, some of them were probably secret police working for Mubarak . . . I have no doubt it was organized. They set out to attack people that day and the proof of that was as soon as they wanted it to stop, it just evaporated."

That same day, Cooper was even more direct in an episode of his CNN public affairs program *Anderson Cooper 360*. He told his viewers: "We're again devoting nearly the entire hour to Egypt, the entire hour to debunking the lies the Egyptian regime continues to try to spread about what is really happening there."

Cooper's post-Egypt commentaries were so dramatic that my former *Los Angeles Times* colleague James Rainey felt the need to make special note of it. In his "On the Media" column, Rainey tallied that Cooper used some variation on the words "lies, lying, or liars" fourteen separate times to describe Mubarak and his regime in a single one-hour program.

In the United States, Cooper's comments sparked some limited criticism that he had abandoned objectivity and launched a personal vendetta against Mubarak after getting beaten up. But Mahmoud Salem credits Cooper with helping turn the tide of American public opinion at a time when many Americans still viewed Mubarak as a solid U.S. ally and important regional peacekeeper.

"Anderson deserves Egyptian nationality," Salem said, laughing.

Just as important as the effect on public opinion, the two-day surge in violence transformed Tahrir itself—hardening the wills and resolve of the people inside. The square became fortified, mentally and physically. Kassem described the Battle of the Camel as a personal point of no return for himself and many others. After that, he said he realized that "couldn't live with it" if the revolution failed.

"After that day, no one was going to leave Tahrir with Mubarak still in power," said Wael Khalil.

On Wednesday morning, Tahrir had felt like a utopian street party. Within forty-eight hours, that feeling had changed to one of paranoia, anger, and back-to-the-wall defiance. It was a fitting two-day microcosm of a fast-moving saga that was marked, as much as anything, by rapid, jarring shifts in tone.

As one female protester told Al Jazeera on Thursday morning, "We know that if we leave now, they'll just hunt us down one by one."

12

The Golden Age of the
Republic of Tahrir

When the protesters took lasting hold of Tahrir Square on January 28, something was unleashed. Reservoirs of confidence, creativity, and empowerment emerged which some feared had been lost forever. Seeing Egyptians regain that sense of dignity, pride, and ownership was one of the most amazing aspects of the entire pressurized three-week Egyptian revolution.

Protester-held Tahrir Square became a sort of utopian ministate. Despite the crowds and the large number of female protesters, the modern Egyptian plague of sexual harassment never entered the square during the revolution. Protesters of widely divergent political views and social circumstances combined to create something truly unique. They organized divisions of labor, arranged their own security details, and diligently cleaned up after themselves. I must have entered Tahrir more than a dozen times, and every single time the streets were cleaner than the street outside my apartment in Giza has ever been.

Every day seemingly revealed new chants, fresh details and bursts of borderline surrealist whimsy. This may have been one of the funniest revolutions in history. Tragically, some of the greatest chants and signs are so deeply rooted in Egyptian slang that they almost defy graceful translation. Egyptians are natural wordsmiths, who love to play with the language in any circumstance. I've literally spent hours debating with friends how to translate this or that chant in a way that would properly convey its essence. My single favorite chant was a good example. In Arabic, it goes, *"Erhal ba, ya aam/khalee aandak dam."* It translates very loosely as "Leave already dude/don't be such a jerk!" But that doesn't come close to capturing its earthy Egyptian hilarity.

I remember a middle-aged man who decided to show up every day wearing a referee's uniform and waving a red card to symbolize that Mubarak and his regime had been ejected from the game. One clever youth summed things up with a simple sign that pleaded, "Just leave already, my arm hurts!" Another had a variation on that theme: "Please leave, I really miss my fiancée!"

One day, Tarek Shalaby met a man holding an anti-Mubarak sign upside down. He informed the man of his apparent mistake and was told with a grin, "Well I've been holding it right-side-up for a week and Mubarak still doesn't understand, so I thought I would try this instead."

On February 10, the day Mubarak delivered his final

speech, a revolutionary art installation was in progress. Near the Egyptian Museum, several people had gathered piles of the rocks and concrete chunks they had used to defend their lives a week earlier. On the ground they were assembling the stones to spell out in huge letters "Leave!" in as many languages they could think of. In addition to the obligatory Arabic, English, and French, there was Spanish, Italian, and even Hebrew. My wife speaks Greek, so she wrote out for them the Greek word and the volunteers joyously set to work adding to their piece.

Multiple stages were assembled for concerts, speeches, and poetry readings; tent cities mushroomed. When the Internet returned, somebody set up a pair of wireless networks called Revolution 1 and Revolution 2. Others assembled a video system and showed movies late at night on an improvised bedsheet screen. The music, drumming, and chanting started and became an alarm clock, starting up about eight in the morning and persisting throughout the day.

By February 5, the utopian republic of Tahrir had been physically and mentally transformed into Fortress Tahrir.

Formidable metal barricades walled off every one of the many roads leading into the square. Men patrolling the edges wore hard hats. Piles of rocks and concrete chunks lay preassembled and waiting to be thrown. On Kasr al-Nil Street a few doors down from After Eight, one of Cairo's most posh and popular nightspots, a medieval trebuchet had been assembled—which, given the mounted cavalry charge they had endured two days earlier, seemed entirely fitting. Whenever the call to prayer rang out, Christian and non-devout Muslim protesters would instinctively flock to the multiple entrances to Tahrir to guard against attack while the devout Muslims conducted their mass open-air prayers.

The crowds had swelled again, as tens of thousands flooded in—many of them vowing never to leave the square vulnerable again. There were now half a dozen different makeshift medical clinics—each stocked with fresh supplies.

The security procedures on the perimeter, which were always fairly robust, had been turned up several notches as well. Just entering Tahrir required running a gauntlet of multiple redundant ID checks and pat-downs by volunteer security wearing their own laminated badges on lanyards around their necks.

The searches of those entering the square were incredibly thorough and exceedingly polite. During that final week of the revolution, Tahrir Square was more secure than most international airports. On February 5, after a traumatic and violent two days, the buoyant mood that marked the early days of the sit-in had also returned. Once you made it through all the security procedures, you were greeted by a clapping and cheering crowd welcoming you to "liberated ground."

There was a new and slightly nasty edge on display as well. El Dahshan recalls visiting the offices of a local travel agency that had been turned into a revolutionary command center on February 3, the day after Tahrir was besieged. There sitting on the floor was one of the captured attackers from the previous day. The man's hands were bound behind his back and his T-shirt was tied around his eyes. Scrawled on his bare chest in ballpoint pen was: "State Security Dog."

The protesters had survived a harrowing experience, just barely, by many accounts, and emerged battered but on their feet. There was a feeling that the regime had played one of its few remaining cards and failed. They knew at this point that (barring some sort of army-led massacre) it was just a matter of time.

On the night of February 7, there came an iconic revolutionary moment. Wael Ghonim, one of the secret planners of the revolt, was released after spending twelve days in detention. A Dubai-based executive for Google, Ghonim had anonymously created the Facebook page "We are all Khaled Saieed" in honor of the notorious victim of police brutality. He had come from Dubai to take part in the first demonstrations, but disappeared into the bowels of the police state on January 28. As the days of his detention grew, supporters and friends revealed to the world Ghonim's true role in the revolution in order to increase public pressure. By the time he was released, he had gained international celebrity status.

Just hours after his release, Ghonim appeared on a popular satellite talk show on the independent channel Dream TV. His raw, painfully sincere performance mesmerized the country.

"We are not traitors," he declared. "We did this because we love Egypt."

Ghonim, thirty-one, wept openly when informed of the estimated three hundred protesters—mostly young people—who had been killed. "It's not our fault," he sobbed before abruptly leaving the studio. "It's the fault of all those who are clinging to power."

Ghonim's interview was particularly crucial because for many Egyptians, it represented the first real mainstreaming of the protesters' message and true face. My elderly Egyptian aunties, for example, generally don't read anything but the state-run *Al-Ahram* newspaper. But they all watch Dream TV. On the day after Ghonim's interview, the already robust numbers in Tahrir spiked visibly.

13

Al Jazeera Under Siege

Covering the Egyptian revolution was a hard enough challenge for most journalists. But for the employees of the Jazeera news channel, it was a particularly harrowing experience. From the very first day, state media and government officials seemed nearly obsessed with Jazeera—openly labeling the Qatar-based network an enemy of the state and a conduit for foreign conspiracies to destabilize Egypt.

"It was just constant harassment," said producer Adam Makary. "It was always a problem being Al Jazeera."

The channel's journalists spent much of the eighteen-day revolution living in a state of perpetual siege, afraid to go home or use their official office for fear of being arrested, and terrified of actually identifying themselves to anybody outside of Tahrir Square. On January 30, representatives of the Ministry of Information raided the channel's offices, confiscating press cards and warning them to cease broadcasting. Employees of Al Jazeera International, the English-language channel, abandoned their office completely and moved operations to a nearby hotel—where they constantly feared the hotel staff would turn them over to the authorities.

By the second day of the revolution, Cairo Bureau Chief Ayman Mohieldin had given up all hope of working normally and formed what he laughingly calls, "a rogue unit." He and a camerawoman simply spent all their time in Tahrir Square broadcasting via a portable satellite phone. For several days he reported only as an unnamed correspondent, broadcasting from an undisclosed location. Throughout the revolution, Mohieldin would receive warnings from other journalists, saying they had been stopped at a checkpoint by police or army officers who were asking for him by name. On February 6, he was detained and blindfolded for several hours after being caught at an army checkpoint trying to enter Tahrir.

At all times, the correspondents and producers lived in mortal fear of being recognized or associated with Al Jazeera. "I was so scared that anyone would know who I work for," said producer Nadia Aboul Magd, a veteran Cairo journalist. Aboul Magd recalls coming to work at the new temporary offices in the Ramsis Hilton, and having to cross through crowds of armed pro-Mubarak supporters chanting, "Where is Jazeera?"

Correspondent Sherine Tadros recalls a bone-chilling moment when she was recognized from television. It was February 2, the night that the pro-Mubarak crowds attacked Tahrir Square. She had taken shelter with a family near the square, identifying herself as a journalist from a fictional European network. Tadros was eating dinner with her temporary host family as the battles raged two blocks away. The television was tuned to the primary state-owned channel, broadcasting a series of street interviews with citizens saying things like "Al Jazeera is saying bad things about Egypt and people in other countries are watching and thinking bad things about Egypt."

Almost on cue, a friend of the family walked in the room; they told him she was a journalist taking shelter and he said, "Oh I know you. I remember your face. You're Sherine from Jazeera English."

The newcomer wasn't angry or accusatory, Tadros recalled. He actually seemed friendly and proud of having made the connection. Still she froze, practically in mid-mouthful, and excused herself to go to the bathroom, then slipped quietly out the door and into the street.

In Alexandria, correspondent Rawya Rageh and her team faced an even more frightening prospect. Rageh, producer Adam Makary, and a cameraman spent a terrified night literally trapped in an apartment building while an enraged machete-wielding crowd gathered in the street outside screaming for Al Jazeera to come out and searching door-to-door.

On February 1, the night of Mubarak's second speech, Rageh decided to set up a remote broadcasting location on a rooftop overlooking Railroad Station Square, an informal gathering point for Alexandria's revolutionary protesters. As a general rule, the Jazeera crew made a point of obscuring their identity. She and Makary were going door-to-door in an apartment building overlooking the square, seeking out a family willing to provide them rooftop or balcony access.

"As we were approaching the door to one apartment, we noticed there was some sign in the hallway that said 'Al Jazeera,'" Makary said. "The sign had no connection to the channel. It was an ad for some other company. But we decided to take it as a good omen."

A working class family opened the door to their modest one-bedroom apartment and asked them what channel they worked for. Rageh, bolstered by the hallway sign, decided to tell the truth.

For several hours, they filmed the scene from the building's rooftop without incident. Then suddenly, shortly after Mubarak finished his speech, a crowd of pro-Mubarak protesters gathered and rushed toward Railroad Station Square. This was the first real violence between the revolutionaries and the pro-Mubarak protesters, taking place more than twelve hours before the time that Tahrir would be attacked. The crowds in Railroad Station Square had never been as large as those in Tahrir, and the revolutionaries there were quickly overwhelmed and defeated by the encroaching pro-Mubarak forces. Jazeera broadcast the entire conflict live, with Rageh narrating. The main Arabic Jazeera channel picked up Rageh's live feed, exponentially expanding its audience. But shortly after the Arabic channel started broadcasting their feed, Rageh and her crew realized they were in danger. The thug squads on the ground had apparently been alerted that they were being filmed and headed straight for the cluster of buildings.

"It was clear the live shot had been going on for too long and they could identify the general area where it was coming from," Rageh said.

An angry, armed crowd gathered in the street outside yelling, "Send out the Jazeera sons of bitches!" The thugs couldn't tell which apartment building the broadcasts had been coming from, so they started going door-to-door. When the knock came on their apartment door, Rageh's impromptu host family lied to protect them, while she and her crew hid behind a bed in another room, and Rageh whispered over the phone to her editors in Qatar.

After a sleepless night, the crowds blocking the building's entrance had thinned a bit and they decided to make a break for it. Rageh donned an Islamic veil as a disguise and made it to safety, but Makary and the cameraman weren't so lucky. The crowds grabbed them and searched their bags, found the camera, and started to attack the journalists. Fortunately the main ringleaders had left by then and the remaining thugs let them go in exchange for a several-hundred-pound payoff.

Rageh and her team returned to Cairo, and she spent the next several nights on the run, staying off the air and sleeping at friends' apartments—afraid to return home.

14

"We Need to Drag Him from His Castle"

It's somehow fitting that Hosni Mubarak's last public act as president of the Republic of Egypt was to infuriate almost everyone and conclusively demonstrate to his citizens that he was not listening.

On February 10, a flurry of early evening developments stoked anticipation that this would be the night that Mubarak would finally surrender and announce his immediate resignation. State television announced that Mubarak would address the nation at 10:00 P.M., and several respectable news outlets reported that Mubarak would resign. I watched the speech on a projection screen in Tahrir along with tens of thousands of deliriously happy protesters. The mood was euphoric. In one section of the vast public space, a group of flag-draped young men danced around in a sort of modified conga line chanting, "Hosni's leaving tonight! Hosni's leaving tonight." Elsewhere a second circle danced and chanted to a live drum as a young man sitting on someone's shoulders led them in chants of: "We're the Internet youth/We're the youth of freedom."

Mubarak's final speech to his people started out on a reasonably promising note. He seemed conciliatory, promising a speech from his heart, a speech of a father to his sons and daughters.

"I would like to tell you that I am proud of you as a symbol of a new generation of Egyptians that is calling for a better change."

But to the crowd's mounting dismay, what followed was an extended, slightly whiny recap of his proud achievements in the service of the nation.

"Like the youth of Egypt today, I was a young man as well when I joined the military and when I pledged loyalty to the nation and sacrifice to the nation. I spent my life defending Egypt's land and sovereignty. I saw its wars, its defeats, and victories. I lived days of occupation and frustration and days of liberation.

"Those were the best days. The best day of my life is when I raised the flag of Egypt over the Sinai," he said. "My aim was never to seek power. I believe that the majority of Egyptian people know who Hosni Mubarak is, and it pains me what has been expressed by some people from my own country."

Mubarak vowed once again to stay in command until his term finished in the fall, so as to oversee the coming transition. He promised dialogue and reform. Shamelessly, he expressed deep sympathy for the families of those killed and injured by his own supporters in the previous week's violence, promising harsh prosecution of those responsible. In short, he offered the protesters absolutely nothing new.

As the president's speech went on and he failed to say the magic sentence everyone was waiting for, there was a sense of stunned realization settling over the crowds. Even the dozen soldiers clustered on top of a nearby tank watching the speech seemed grim.

About halfway through Mubarak's message, one spectator yelled out: "Does that look like someone who's leaving? He won't go until he's removed. So we'll remove him!"

The mood in the immediate aftermath of Mubarak's speech was difficult to define—equal parts deflation, determination, and a mounting sense of pure rage. Within seconds of his conclusion, the multiple video screens in Tahrir were struck by a hail of hurled shoes and sandals.

"I feel hatred. I feel like we need to drag him from his palace," said Mayada Moursi, a schoolteacher in her early thirties.

Even in the final hours of the Mubarak era, I was concerned about publishing the open treason of Moursi's statements. At the end of our interview, I asked Moursi if she wanted her name published or preferred the safety of anonymity. Her husband urged anonymity, but she laughed and overruled him. She had crossed her own personal point of no return regarding the man who had ruled over most of her life.

Another protester, when I asked his immediate feelings, simply shrugged and told me, "I feel like our president is stupid."

Crucially, the U.S. government sounded equally fed-up. The Obama administration had been dropping hints to the Washington, D.C., press corps all day that a historic change was coming, and they clearly expected that Mubarak would be stepping down. Whether they misinterpreted the signals or were openly misled by Mubarak remains one of the revolution's final mysteries. Obama's subsequent statement made it clear whose side his administration was on. He praised the protesters who "have exercised their right to peaceful assembly, represent the greatness of the Egyptian people, and are broadly representative of Egyptian society," and flatly accused Mubarak of stalling and dragging out the process. "The Egyptian government must put forward a credible, concrete, and unequivocal path toward genuine democracy, and they have not yet seized that opportunity," Obama said.

The next day, enraged and inspired by Mubarak's enduring stubbornness, the protesters staked out new ground. One group moved to surround the Information Ministry a short distance from Tahrir—home of the state-run television channels. A second group of protesters made the several-mile trek to the presidential palace in the outlying district of Heliopolis. The army surrounded and secured each building, but made no move to disperse any of the protesters. The military also started issuing official communiqués, promising that no protesters would be attacked and that the emergency laws would be repealed as soon as possible. The sudden appearance of military com-muniqués historically means only one thing in a Middle Eastern context: a coup.

According to several Egyptians I spoke with that day, the statements coming out of the military, and the way they were titled and structured, were proof that an army power play against Mubarak was either in prog-ress or had already happened

Finally at about six in the evening, a grim Vice-President Suleiman read a terse statement on state television that Mubarak had resigned and left power to the Supreme Armed Forces Council.

It was over.

15

"One Hand" Divided

With Mubarak deposed and in seclusion in the presidential compound in Sharm al-Shiekh, Egypt suddenly found itself governed by the Supreme Council for the Armed Forces or SCAF—a little known grouping of senior generals led by long-serving Defense Minister Field Marshall Mohammed Hussein Tantawi. What started as a popular mass uprising had ended with a palace coup. Few people even knew exactly who composed the SCAF, beyond a few well-known names, but the council began its reign amid an air of good will over the restraint displayed by the military during the revolution.

But almost as soon as Mubarak left the stage, the relationship between the primary activist groups and SCAF started coming under stress. Critics charged this council of generals with openly dragging its feet on genuine structural reform. The universally demanded purge and overhaul of the Interior Ministry proved to be shallow and cosmetic. A few dozen senior police generals were pushed into early retirement and a few more were shuffled into different positions. But the basic structure of Mubarak's police state remained unchanged. What's worse, the country's new military rulers appeared to be turning a blind eye to a systematic campaign by the remnants of State Security to destroy incriminating evidence that could be used against the agency in postrevolution trials.

"All those guys in State Security are still hanging around. We haven't even changed the personalities, let alone the system, and these people are still, in my view, very resentful over what happened," Mohammed ElBaradei told me. "My theory is that State Security has files against everybody. Nobody is able to hit them hard because they have enough information on everybody. I can't see any other reason why you just don't get and train a completely new set of people."

In early March, fueled by rumors of this ongoing State Security cover-up effort, protesters started taking matters into their own hands. Angry crowds overran and invaded State Security buildings in Alexandria and Cairo. In each case, they found mountains of freshly shredded documents. A similar attempt to overrun the Ministry of Interior itself, just outside of Tahrir Square, was violently beaten back by army soldiers firing live ammunition into the air and wielding batons.

It wasn't just the activist groups who were losing patience with the military's handling of post-Mubarak Egypt. The SCAF and its troops on the ground also seemed to become deeply fed up with the ongoing protests. The generals, who continued to rule via communiqué, appeared to be remarkably thin-skinned regarding any sort of public criticism. Several journalists and commentators who criticized their decisions were summoned for questioning. At one point, Asmaa Mahfouz, the young woman who achieved YouTube fame prior to the revolution, faced defamation and incitement charges for posting a Facebook message that criticized the SCAF. Military censors began monitoring state television and newspapers to ensure the SCAF was treated respectfully.

Alaa Al Aswany, author of *The Yacoubian Building* and a longtime political columnist, theorized that the career military men who constitute the SCAF simply didn't have the background or mind-set to handle being thrust into a raucous newly democratic situation like post-Mubarak Egypt.

"You're talking about a military mentality. It's the first time anyone has tried to discuss anything with them," Al Aswany said. "A normal military general, he's either giving orders or receiving orders and carrying them out. The idea that we can sit down together and I can tell them, 'This decision was wrong,' it's outside of their culture."

The SCAF's frustration with the ongoing protests appeared to bubble over in March, resulting in a shameful incident that recalled the worst human rights abuses of the Mubarak era. On March 9, soldiers forcibly broke up a planned protest in Tahrir, arresting dozens of activists and imprisoning them on the grounds of the Egyptian Museum. Detainees later reported that they were beaten, strip-searched and subjected to electric shocks. Eighteen female protesters were detained and several of them were forcibly subjected to "virginity tests."

Twenty-year-old Salwa Hosseini was one of the victims of these tests, and she told of her experiences in an interview with the *Los Angeles Times*. She said the soldiers beat her and several other female detainees, called them prostitutes, and attempted to take pictures of them after they had been stripped. When she protested, she was shocked with a stun gun. Despite Hosseini's request that the forced vaginal exam be at least performed by a female doctor in private, it was done by a male doctor, "in front of guards and military officers," she said. Perhaps the most disturbing detail was the aftermath; when Hosseini went public with her allegations, she said, "People didn't believe us. Some people think the military is like their parents. If this hadn't happened to me, I wouldn't believe it either."

Hosseini's testimony reflected a problem faced by many of the postrevolution activists who, through ongoing street action, sought to keep up pressure on the SCAF. While activist groups were willing to continue confronting the generals to ensure that their revolutionary demands were met, a large section of the Egyptian population seemed desperate to trust the SCAF and fearful of further instability. In May, stand-up comedian Adham Abdel Salam summed up the national mood: "Our relationship with the army is that of a woman with the husband she knows cheats on her—but she won't say anything because she's worried about the kids."

Over the spring of 2011, a clear and unhealthy pattern developed. The SCAF would concede as little as possible in terms of actual on-the-ground reform, only making major concessions under threat of renewed mass protests. One glaring example of this dynamic was the postrevolution arrests and trials of regime figures. Smaller fish were immediately arrested, such as former Information Minister Anas Al-Fiqi, former Tourism Minister Zoheir Garana and Ahmed Ezz, the steel tycoon, who rose to power as a protégé of Gamal Mubarak. All three were rapidly railroaded into courtroom cages and sentenced for a variety of corruption charges. But Mubarak and his sons Gamal and Alaa remained at large for months, as did a trio of senior regime lieutenants—Safwat al-Sherif, former presidential chief of staff Zakaria Azmi and longtime Parliament speaker Fathi Surour. It wasn't until early April, nearly two months after the regime's collapse, that authorities issued arrest warrants for these men—and that was only in response to a new wave of Tahrir protests demanding their incarceration.

"They didn't want to put Mubarak on trial," said Hani Shukrallah, editor of *Al-Ahram Online*, the state newspaper's English-language portal Web site. "SCAF has wanted to stop the revolution at every single juncture."

Plans for the eventual transition to democratic rule became a major and ongoing point of contention. In a March 19 national referendum, Egyptians overwhelmingly approved a package of constitutional amendments that put the country on a fast-track schedule toward parliamentary elections in autumn 2011. Most secular activist groups came out strongly against the referendum because it put elections ahead of the drafting of a new constitution. But the SCAF and the Muslim Brotherhood both campaigned hard in favor, arguing that the rapid elections offered the fastest possible return to normality. Critics charged that they were simply trotting out a new version of the Mubarak-era "stability above all else" argument to exploit the fears of a nervous populace.

Another serious point of contention fueling this second wave of anti-SCAF protests was the army's newfound passion for military tribunals. Local human rights groups estimated that in the eight months following Mubarak's resignation, twelve thousand civilians were sentenced in military trials for offenses ranging from "incitement to violence" (or, unacceptable political activism) to common street crimes. Each new confrontation between protesters and increasingly aggressive soldiers only added to this poisonous atmosphere. By midsummer, anti-SCAF sentiment was peaking. In July, activists staged a second long-term occupation of Tahrir that lasted nearly a month. The list of demands included a firm timeline for democratic transition, the end of military trials for civilians, and a sincere purging of Mubarak-era cronies from a host of institutions ranging from the Interior Ministry to the state media and the ranks of university deans. New tent cities and stages sprung up as the protesters tried to revive that old revolutionary spirit from the golden age of Tahrir, just months earlier. But this second occupation proved a bit of a disaster. For starters, there was ongoing divisiveness among the activist groups. In the original revolution, the disparate political groups managed to put aside competing agendas and allegiances for the sake of the larger common goal. But in the July sit-in, these divisions were on full display as each group seemed to have its own banners, tents, and stages. Meanwhile, the SCAF succeeded in using the media to paint the protesters as fanatics who were holding up the country's return to normality.

By August, at the start of the Muslim fasting month of Ramadan, the slightly demoralized activist ranks agreed to pack up and go home. Army soldiers and a reconstituted Central Security violently rounded up the stragglers and temporarily declared Tahrir Square a political action-free zone. When activists attempted to hold a public Iftar (the fast-breaking Ramadan sunset meal) in the square, they were immediately pounced upon and dispersed by security.

Wael Khalil, the veteran socialist activist, describes this failed second occupation of Tahrir as a well-meaning mistake, believing that the protesters simply overstayed their welcome in the square and failed to articulate their goals to the wider population.

"It was very good in the first week. We had good numbers and a clear message," he said. "It could have wrapped up after that first week and we would have maximized the gains."

By week three of the occupation—amid growing divisiveness and tension—a consensus was forming among the protesters to leave. But this internal debate was "totally monopolized and dominated by loud voices," Khalil said. Others, he said, were afraid they would be regarded as soft on revolution or disloyal to the blood of its martyrs if they didn't stay.

In September 2011, Google executive Wael Ghonim made headlines by writing an open letter directly addressed to Field Marshal Tantawi. Ghonim's letter criticized the pace of reform, the absence of transparency and true dialogue, and the lack of a definitive transitional timetable.

"More groups of youth become frustrated with every day that passes without a clear road map and fundamental changes in the way our nation is being governed. Some of them feel compelled to escalate matters," Ghonim wrote. "There is a historical opportunity now for the SCAF to work with the people who have awakened and revolted in order to set Egypt on the right track . . . We want you to believe in the Egyptian youth who have earned the world's admiration for their revolution. We want you to believe that they have many solutions and to give them their deserved opportunity to lead the nation."

His complaints were not new, but the source was significant. Ghonim was one of the most prominent voices among the hard-core Tahrir activists to still profess faith in SCAF leadership, long after many of his compatriots had turned against the generals. In the aftermath of the revolution, many of his fellow revolutionaries wrote Ghonim off as a SCAF apologist. His late emergence as a public critic heralded a potentially volatile new phase.

In June, I had attended a Reuters-sponsored conference in London that featured several seminars on the Arab Spring. One such session featured two young Egyptian revolutionaries speaking live, and Ghonim participating via video conference from Dubai. The other Egyptians were highly critical of the SCAF's performance thus far and openly predicting a fresh set of confrontations. But Ghonim was on a completely different page from the start. "I still trust the SCAF," he told the attendees, as his fellow revolutionaries in the room rolled their eyes in frustration. "They haven't done anything yet to cause me to lose faith in them."

As a summer of discontent drew to a close, a distinct air of gloom and pessimism seemed to take hold. In addition to what seemed to be a looming new confrontation with SCAF, crime was on the rise, the economy was still sputtering, and the newfound freedom of expression seemed to produce little more than shouted accusations on all sides of the political spectrum. Fears of a post-Mubarak regression to authoritarianism were only heightened by a renewed late-summer SCAF push to tighten controls on the media and suppress dissent. In September, the government announced it was freezing all new licenses for private satellite television stations and would begin closely monitoring the behavior of the media. New Minister of Information Ossama Heikal invoked Mubarak-era rhetoric in promising that any newspaper or channel that "endangers the stability and security of the country" would be firmly dealt with. Heikal said the government and military council respect "freedom of the media and press, but without infringing on social morality and national principles," and would not allow any media outlet to "agitate citizens and incite violence."

The media push was accompanied by a surprise an-
nouncement that the reviled Emergency Laws would be
dusted off and applied in the case of a variety of new offenses, including spreading dangerous rumors and blocking public streets with protests. General Mamdouh
Shaheen, the SCAF's spokesman, defended the move in a
television appearance as "necessary to restore order and
stability. . . . What we are seeing on the Egyptian street is
terrorism. Firm measures are needed to curb the violence."

The Mubarak-era suspicion of Jazeera even carried over
into the new Egypt; security forces repeatedly raided the
offices of Jazeera Mubasher Misr (Jazeera Live Egypt),
a specialized 24/7 Egyptian news channel that Jazeera
founded after the revolution.

Internal societal divisions continued to emerge under
the SCAF's rule, stoking fears of widening sectarian unrest and (in the minds of many Egyptians) justifying the
military's harsh grip on the country. In early October
a succession of sectarian incidents resulted in bloody
clashes that left more than a dozen Christians dead. After
a Coptic church was attacked in the southern city of As-
wan, thousands of Christians marched to the state television building demanding greater protection from the
government. According to multiple eyewitness accounts,
the marchers were attacked by both ordinary plain-
clothed citizens and the army, which allegedly ran over
protesters with tanks and armored vehicles. At least
twenty-four were killed and hundreds wounded.

After the debacle of the virginity tests, further evidence emerged to indicate the brutal internal culture of

the Interior Ministry wasn't just restricted to the police. In September, a widely circulated Internet video showed a large crowd of uniformed military officers harshly bullying a pair of terrified men. The victims—suspected weapons dealers in the Nile Delta province of Dakahliya—were repeatedly beaten on the head and neck and shocked with a stun gun. Military officials promised a swift investigation, but the incident proved how little had actually changed in Egypt's criminal justice system.

But despite the multiple setbacks, some people remained cautiously optimistic, describing Egypt's rocky first post-Mubarak months as a necessary process. ElBaradei theorized that the Mubarak years had essentially stunted the Egyptian psyche and sense of community. The end result was a people that simply didn't know how to handle complex issues and ideological or sectarian differences without resorting to accusations, hysteria, and violence.

"The older generation like me, with very few exceptions, are a liability right now. . . . It's not a group of people who are really buying into democracy. And that's not surprising. These people have been working for years and years under autocratic rule. They're not going to wake up the next day and become democrats," ElBaradei said. "What you're seeing now is a lot of pus coming out of the wound. It's natural and it has to happen before the real healing can begin."

Among the activists, a healthy debate developed as to whether the SCAF was being incompetent or actively devious. Were they bungling the postrevolutionary process or were they trying to sabotage it? Speculation grew that the generals sought to muddy the transitional waters in order to justify staying in power. That rumor was partially fueled by the actions of Field Marshal Tantawi himself, who started to openly boost his public profile—giving speeches and presiding over the opening of factories. In late September, Tantawi made a surprise public walking tour of downtown Cairo dressed in a civilian suit, shaking hands with citizens and generally acting like a man running for political office. In a subsequent speech, he dismissed talk of his presidential ambitions as, "only rumors and we shouldn't waste time talking about rumors." Tantawi denied any intention by the military to lengthen their period in power. But he ominously added, "We will not leave Egypt until we have fulfilled all we promised and do our duty towards the people."

Many, however, remained confident that the SCAF could not derail the transition to democracy—even if they wanted to.

"The Military Council is not going to rule Egypt. If they try, they're making a fatal mistake," Al Aswany said. "There's an element that has changed, the most important element—the Egyptian people. They will never accept it again."

Shukrallah, the *Al-Ahram* editor, speculated that the SCAF's primary concern was stage-managing the transition in a way that ensures that the military, and its budget and perks, remained untouchable and independent of any civilian authority—an example of the so-called "Turkish Model" where the military remains a separate institution free from civilian oversight.

"Once the democracy starts working, their role retreats more and more," Shukrallah said. "They will go. I'm not worried about that. But hopefully they won't leave the country in a total mess."

One senior general, an advisor to the SCAF but not an official member of the council, essentially confirmed that strategy in an interview with *The Washington Post*. Speaking anonymously, the general described this scenario as necessary to ensure that Islamist forces don't rise to dominate post-Mubarak Egypt. The unspoken implication was that the military would retain the right to step in and overthrow any elected government that it deemed was straying from the proper path.

"We want a model like Turkey, but we won't force it," the general said. "Egypt as a country needs this to protect our democracy from the Islamists. We know this group doesn't think democratically."

16

The Bearded Hordes

The long-suffering members of the Muslim Brotherhood can be forgiven for thoroughly enjoying their postrevolutionary moment in the sun. Immediately after Mubarak's departure, the Brotherhood embarked on what amounted to an extended public coming-out party. They opened a massive new headquarters, in a ceremony covered by the media; they formed an official political party called Freedom and Justice; senior officials started appearing regularly on television; and foreign government delegations (including U.S. government officials) began seeking out Brotherhood leaders for meetings. It was basically a several-months-long victory lap.

"It has been a big difference," said Mohammed al-Beltagy, a senior Brotherhood official who essentially lived in Tahrir Square and served as the group's on-the-ground field commander for the entirety of the revolution. "It's not just that I'm happy to go on state television or have *Al-Ahram* quote me or publish my editorials. The real goal is to have true parliamentary institutions, a true independent press, truly independent judges, [a] true civil society, true sovereignty of law and [a] real, honorable constitution. That will be the big difference."

The future of the Brotherhood, and of other Islamist movements, was one of the primary questions hanging over the country's future. Much of the West, and a healthy percentage of secular and Christian Egyptians, seem genuinely frightened that the removal of the dictatorship will herald the immediate rise of an Islamic Republic of Egypt. This was, of course, the Mubarak party line for decades.

"The panic over the Muslim Brotherhood was the strategy of the old regime to delay any democratic development," al-Beltagy said. "That's still being used by parties inside and outside the country."

The worst-case scenario now seemed to be a vision of the largest and most influential Arab country morphing into a fanatical citadel on Israel's borders—one that tears up the Camp David Peace Accords and begins aggressively exporting militant Islam throughout the region.

But the truth on the ground is far more complicated. The Muslim Brotherhood's political strength remains an open question simply because its previous successes took place in a different Egypt. They excelled largely because they cared the most in an apolitical and demoralized playing field. Put simply, they were the only players on the political spectrum willing to risk beatings and imprisonment in order to vote. Normal citizens generally stayed home and secular-liberal political activists mostly boycotted the process and focused their energies on street protests.

The Muslim Brotherhood's prospects in a politicized Egypt are much murkier. They will certainly occupy a position of influence in all parliaments going forward. With clear, widespread grassroots support and after decades of open persecution for their beliefs, it's hard to argue that they don't deserve it. But for the first time in living memory, they will have real competition at the polling places.

"We may have the Muslim Brotherhood forming the next government, but there will be no Islamic Republic of Egypt," said Hani Shukrallah, who joined the newly formed leftist Social Democrat Party after the revolution. He estimated that the Brotherhood's historic victories in the 2005 parliamentary elections took place among 10 to 15 percent voter turnout, and he expects that number to be more than 50 percent in all forthcoming elections.

One indicator of the new Egyptian political climate: a host of smaller elections for university students and professional unions took place in the summer of 2011, with decidedly mixed results for the Brotherhood. Throughout the 1990s, the Brotherhood staged effective power plays at a number of professional syndicates, similar to the manner in which the Christian Coalition targeted American school boards during the Reagan years. Right up until the revolution, the Doctors' Syndicate was essentially Brotherhood territory. Senior Brotherhood officials made up most of the administration; they would be arrested in periodic crackdowns, then emerge smiling from jail and head right back to their prior positions.

But the postrevolution syndicate elections tell a different story. Brotherhood candidates dominated elections for the school teachers' union, but were heavily defeated in elections for the internal union of professors at Cairo's Ain Shams University.

"We appreciate that there is competition now," al-Beltagy said. "We win in some places and lose in others."

In addition to renewed competition from outside, the Brotherhood faces unfamiliar challenges from within. It's easy to retain group unity during a struggle against an overarching enemy, but much harder in a postrevolutionary environment when long-suppressed internal divisions come to the forefront.

Several prominent younger members broke away from the group after the revolution, complaining that the Brotherhood's decision making was dominated by an opaque council of elderly autocrats who left no room for new thinking. The end result has been a splintering of the Islamist ranks that could provide more opportunity for nascent liberal and secular forces to enter the parliament. Islam Lotfy, a young Islamist human rights lawyer, split off to form his own party, the Islamic Current. In a series of interviews, Lotfy described the Brotherhood as "out of touch" and dominated by septuagenarians, who will keep "doing things the same way for the rest of their lives."

Another factor that could affect the Muslim Brotherhood's post-Mubarak honeymoon is corruption. Retaining a noble and incorruptible reputation is one thing when you're frozen out of power. As of autumn 2011, there were already scattered signs that success was going to the heads of the Muslim Brotherhood's leadership and extended families. In late September, a police lieutenant in the rural province of Sharqeya charged that the son of senior Muslim Brotherhood official Mohammed Moursi had verbally abused him during a routine traffic stop.

There are newer, more radical forces emerging as well to challenge the Brotherhood from the right. The Salafists, extremist Muslims who make the Brotherhood look like moderates, have embraced party politics with the enthusiasm of true fanatics. Many of these groups avoided politics during the Mubarak era, but in the wake of the revolution, at least three different Salafist political parties were founded. Unlike the Brotherhood, these groups openly advocate the institution of mandatory Saudi-style Islamic law and dismiss the possibility that a Christian or a woman could ever serve in a significant leadership position.

Al Aswany claimed he has no problem cooperating with the Muslim Brotherhood on building the new Egypt. But he finds the Salafists impossible to work with.

"It's like they've come in a time machine from the fourteenth century," he said. "They're against books, they're against cinema, they're against everything. You can't tell me that everything is a sin. I'm a Muslim, too."

In an analogy only a professional dentist could pull off, Al Aswany compared Egypt's resurgent Salafists to the "anaerobic bacteria" he finds in a patient's mouth. "It dies as soon as you introduce it to oxygen. That's what democracy is—the oxygen," he said. "Once we have democracy, the Salafists will lose ground."

The fragile unity between Islamists and secularists that characterized the revolution didn't last long after Mubarak's departure. By midsummer, both sides were exchanging recriminations, with the secular activist forces charging that the Muslim Brotherhood was railroading the country into early elections, where they would hold a natural organizational advantage.

"The people who are organized on the ground are the Muslim Brotherhood, who have been working for eighty years, and the remnants of the NDP," Mohammed ElBaradei said. "The new parties that were founded a month ago are not going to have a chance."

ElBaradei warned that if the Brotherhood and other Islamists dominate the first post-Mubarak parliament, it would lead to a corruption of the drafting of the new constitution. He and other secular activists spent much of the summer of 2011 unsuccessfully lobbying the SCAF to impose a supraconstitutional Bill of Rights that would protect the rights of women and religious minorities against just such a possibility.

It was precisely this distrust between the two sides that helped derail the second occupation of Tahrir. On July 29, Islamist forces staged a dramatic power play—overwhelming the square with raucous crowds chanting for the imposition of Sharia (Islamic law). Outraged secular activists decried the move as a blatant betrayal of the spirit of the revolution, and voted to end their sit-in shortly afterward. Wael Khalil described the postrevolutionary tension between secularists and Islamists as something of a false conflict fueled by hysteria and hype. The main challenge going forward, he said, was to "resist this false polarization" driven by fanatics on both sides of the ideological divide.

"The Salafists are scared we'll turn into Sweden and the liberals are afraid we'll turn into Iran," Khalil said. "The choice is not whether to have a country like Iran or a country like Sweden. That's not a real choice."

17

Tearing Down the Propaganda Machine

In retrospect, Shahira Amin knew subconsciously when she left her apartment that she wasn't going to work anymore. A longtime presenter and administrator at Nile TV, the government's foreign-language channel, Amin was scheduled to read the English-language news at 11 P.M., but she left home wearing casual clothing inappropriate for appearing on camera—just jeans and a T-shirt. It was the night of February 3; the battle for Tahrir had finally ended around dawn and the protesters in the square were still tending to their wounds and fortifying in anticipation of further assaults. Elsewhere around the city, dozens of journalists were being attacked. Amin had reached her breaking point, although she wasn't quite ready to admit it to herself yet.

In order to reach the radio and television building she had to pass by Tahrir. But instead of continuing to work, she found herself heading into the square. From there she took the final step, sending a text message to her boss at the channel: "Forgive me, I'm not coming back to the building. I'm on the people's side, not the regime's."

Amin's abrupt resignation was the culmination of a steadily increasing crisis of conscience prompted by the revolution. She had worked at Nile TV since it was founded in 1994, gradually rising through the ranks to become deputy head of the channel. In the process she earned a reputation as an internal troublemaker who consistently pushed for higher journalistic standards at the state-owned mouthpiece.

From the beginning of the protests on January 25, Amin found it nearly impossible to do her job with any degree of professionalism. She hosted a public affairs show on the night of the twenty-fifth and was called into the office of the head of the news division and given a specific set of marching orders. The opposition politician who was scheduled to be her guest was out, and in his place was an NDP parliamentarian. Her mandatory talking points that night would be threefold: the foreign elements organizing the protests; the shadowy hand of the Muslim Brotherhood in stoking the unrest; and the need for all parties to engage in a national dialogue.

"It was the worst interview of my life," Amin said. "I went home feeling sick and hoping that nobody was watching."

Prior to the interview, Amin and her fellow news anchor were given a press release from the Ministry of the Interior and told to read it out verbatim on the air. The statement insisted there had been no clashes anywhere in the country, but then noted that five people had died in Suez; the press release didn't bother to explain how those five people could possibly have died if there had been no clashes. Amin outright refused to read it, and left her broadcast partner to do the dirty work.

The next day she traveled to London on a prescheduled trip and returned to Egypt on January 30. Her first day back on the air was February 2, the day Tahrir was besieged. Even as footage of the mounted charge into Tahrir was being broadcast around the globe, she was specifically instructed to act as if the attacks taking place ten minutes away had never happened.

"I told them the satellite channels were all showing it, and they said we were not allowed to mention it," Amin said, "I entered the studio really angry . . . I felt like if I stayed one more day I would be committing career suicide and betraying the protesters, these young people putting their lives on the line for our freedom."

As the revolution moved into its final days, senior administrators at state-owned newspapers and television channels found themselves fending off their own internal insurrections. Sabah Hamamou, a deputy business editor for the main state daily *Al-Ahram*, helped lead an internal revolt there—one that demanded mass resignations among the senior editors and called for coverage that reflected the reality taking place on the streets.

But with the exception of isolated dissidents like Amin and Hamamou, Egypt's state-owned empire of newspapers and television channels dutifully did its job almost until the very end—de-emphasizing the size of the crowds in Tahrir, and pushing the line that the protests were led by a sinister combination of Muslim Brothers, shadowy foreign infiltrators, and Jazeera correspondents. About a week into the revolution, the state press could no longer plausibly ignore or downplay the unrest, so it switched tactics. The protests were covered, but the demonstrators' demands were reported as focusing exclusively on corruption and lack of economic opportunity; the primary demand for Mubarak's departure was generally ignored. Commentators on state television started describing the revolution as something that started on January 25 with honorable and noble intentions, but had been hijacked and corrupted by internal and external forces who sought to destabilize Egypt.

On February 4, one of the state news channels—which had been running an Egyptian flag logo in the corner of the screen along with the slogan "protect Egypt"—presented the following investigative scoop.

"Dear viewers, we want to bring you this footage obtained by a patriotic Egyptian in Tahrir Square," the anchor said, according to an article by *Time* magazine's Rania Abouzeid. What followed was a shaky image of a middle-aged blond woman and a young, bearded Western man wearing a trademark Palestinian scarf. The man held a sign that read, "In solidarity with the Egyptian people" written in English.

"It's clear, dear viewers, that there are many foreigners protesting down in Tahrir. These are the people in the square," the presenter concluded.

On February 5, I was contacted by Nile TV—the channel Amin had just quit—to comment on current events. Immediately, the news anchor started pushing the "foreign elements" line, telling me, "We can see quite well that external elements are quite evident and the conspiracy theories going on."

I explained that I had seen absolutely no evidence of foreign influence or involvement, and that Tahrir protesters were "adamant that they don't want any help from outside."

At that point she abruptly ended the interview and concluded, "We don't need any sort of interference in our internal affairs because we are capable of managing it well."

By the time Mubarak resigned, the state media had switched sides with a vengeance—becoming comically pro-revolution. Front-page headlines trumpeted "the fall of the corrupt ones" without a hint of irony, and hailed the achievements of the protesters who had been so recently vilified. In mid-April, *Al-Ahram* reported "widespread national jubilation" and an "overwhelming sense of joy and retribution" at the news that Mubarak and his two sons had been arrested.

"*Al-Ahram* became almost desperately pro-revolution, with the same kind of vulgarity with which they were pro-Mubarak," said Hani Shukrallah, editor of *Al-Ahram Online*. "Basically they realized that there was a new ass they had to kiss."

Neither approach, of course, qualifies as proper journalism, and the state-owned media in the aftermath of the revolution found itself facing a truly existential dilemma. Even under Mubarak, state organs like *Al-Ahram* were already losing ground to private upstarts like *Al-Masry Al-Youm* and *Al-Shorouk* while multiple satellite channels had been chipping away at the influence of state television for years.

That competition is only going to increase. Ibrahim Eissa, the former *Al-Dostour* editor who was blackballed in autumn 2010, returned to prominence immediately after the revolution—editing a new newspaper called *Al-Tahrir* and serving as the centerpiece of a new Tahrir satellite television channel. Kassem, the former *Cairo Times* and *Al-Masry Al-Youm* publisher, is planning to roll out his own independent newspaper as well.

Suddenly state journalists found themselves actually having to compete for readers and viewers, and turn a profit, all while essentially teaching themselves how to be real journalists.

Al-Ahram Online is a curious case study in Egypt's complicated media dynamics. The Web site, which generates unique content from its own dedicated staff along with daily, select translations from the Arabic, debuted just before the November 2010 parliamentary elections and immediately distinguished itself with straightforward reporting that pushed the far boundaries of state-sponsored journalism. Shukrallah himself spent years as the managing editor of the English-language *Al-Ahram Weekly* before jumping to a senior editor position at the privately owned *Al-Shorouk* daily newspaper. (Full disclosure: I briefly worked as a copy editor at the *Weekly* under Shukrallah in the late '90s).

When *Al-Ahram Online* was starting up, Shukrallah was recruited back into state-backed journalism. As one of the few Egyptian journalists to serve in a senior position at both public and private newspapers, he offers a unique perspective on the challenges of reforming Egypt's media scene.

"You look at the media and you find the same paradox that you see in the rest of the country. You can look at Egypt postrevolution and say there's been an enormous, massive sea change. Mubarak is in the dock, the whole gang is behind bars, et cetera," he said. "On the other hand, you still have emergency laws, military trials, Central Security occupying Tahrir Square, and you feel nothing has changed at all."

In the immediate aftermath of Mubarak's February 11 resignation, *Al-Ahram* and other state media institutions were essentially lost at sea and searching for a new identity. This uncertainty produced a slightly schizophrenic reaction.

"For a while, they were totally confused because there was no master, and SCAF had not yet crystallized as the new master. It was a free-for-all. Whoever was sitting on the desk that day determined the policy of the newspaper," Shukrallah said. "When you have this kind of jumble, you get spaces within these institutions where the people who are sincere are able to work."

On a certain level, the postrevolutionary changes were

obvious and positive. For years, state television and newspapers had refused to even speak the name of the Muslim Brotherhood, referring to it only as "the banned group." Now suddenly senior Brotherhood leaders were regular fixtures on state television. Suddenly the discussions taking place on state television channels and editorial pages had become fascinating and vibrant.

But there were just as many parallel signs of how difficult it may be to truly "fix" Egypt's state media— prompting the question of whether or not it's even worth fixing. Efforts by internal reformers within newspapers and television have often been met by fierce resistance, and an eventual return to nepotistic hiring practices and instinctive self-censorship. Tellingly, both Amin and Hamamou, the dissidents from Nile TV and *Al-Ahram,* sound deeply frustrated with the way things have developed.

Al-Ahram's editor in chief, Osama Saraya, was ousted shortly after the revolution. In an e-mail exchange with *Newsweek* magazine, Saraya wrote that his newspaper, "had a strong link with the State system and this is the nature of all the national press. . . . We are victims of the system, we worked under its shadow and we aren't criminals who can be accused of any charges, whether it is from our colleagues or other papers. The responsibility is collective, although I accept my personal responsibility."

But despite Saraya's dismissal, most of the remaining senior editors and section heads at *Al-Ahram* remained in place. When I met with Hamamou in early October, she had just lost a battle to oust her own long-serving business editor—whom she charged had cozy relations with

a host of regime-connected businessmen and received a backdoor cut of the section's advertising revenue. Many of her colleagues, included those who supported the revolution, had rallied to the editor's cause, and Hamamou sensed she was already becoming marginalized as a noisy troublemaker within the newsroom.

"It's going slowly—the same way it's going in the rest of the country," Hamamou said. "There are still many little Mubaraks here at *Al-Ahram*. The place is run like a family farm."

Amin reported similar frustrations at state television, where she returned in an extremely limited role. She now hosts a weekly interview program on one of the Arabic-language channels, where she retains more control over the content and has been able to put senior Muslim Brotherhood officials on the air. But at Nile TV, the channel she helped build, she is persona non grata. Former colleagues, including people she hired and helped groom, now speak bitterly of her for going public to the international media with the reasons for her resignation. Several Nile TV employees, speaking off the record, complained that Amin had embarrassed them and, in the words of one producer, "made a hero out of herself at our expense."

Amin counters that in the absence of sweeping internal reform and mass firings, Egypt's state media is destined to revert to old habits—instinctively self-censoring and defending those in power because that's what they've always done.

"They don't want me back because they know I'll push for change," she said. "What needs to happen now is a total

evaluation. We need to see who can be trained and improved and who has to go immediately. They were all hired for their connections and so many of them are simply not qualified."

Shukrallah, the *Al-Ahram Online* editor, says there are already signs that the state media have responded to the revolution by simply switching masters—becoming shameless cheerleaders for the SCAF instead of shameless cheerleaders for Mubarak's NDP.

"Standards are still bad. Editorial policy is still pro-government, pro-state and pro-SCAF," he said. "They still see their mission as defending the ruling authority, but they're doing it with a much greater degree of openness and sophistication because they know they have to compete now. They are kissing the SCAF's ass but they all realize that the SCAF may not be around within a couple of months. So they're hedging their bets. They can't antagonize anyone because you never know who's going to be governing the country within six months."

However Shukrallah cautions that journalistic standards are not necessarily utopian on the private sector side of the street. Newspapers like *Al-Masry Al-Youm* and *Al-Shorouk* are still young and immature entities built around the whims and business interests of one or two powerful owners. "Compared to a mature joint-stock company, these papers are still basically family grocery stores," he said. Based on his experiences at *Al-Shorouk*, he joked that the newspaper's editorial policies seemed to be guided by "Whoever [owner and publisher] Ibrahim El-Moallem was having dinner with last night."

Kassem's new newspaper, expected to debut in 2012, specifically seeks to fix that problem of a single powerful owner exerting too much influence. According to his business model, no single investor can hold more than a 10 percent stake in the company.

In the end, the problem of how to deal with Egypt state-owned media might end up solving itself through simple economic inertia. Like most public sector enterprises, the state media machine is hideously overstaffed and stocked with thousands of phantom employees drawing a paycheck for barely working. If everyone at *Al-Ahram* or state television actually showed up for work on the same day, it would be chaos. Hamamou estimates that the entire *Al-Ahram* empire, which puts out dozens of different publications, employs as many as eleven thousand people to do a job that could be filled by three thousand properly trained and motivated employees.

Hisham Kassem predicted that the combination of dwindling readership and viewers, along with the massive economic drain of supporting the propaganda machine, would eventually succeed where the internal reformers fail.

"There's going to be a populist demand to shut down these places," he said, "not because they're hypocrites or anything but because we can use the cash."

18

The Reckoning

The arrests started almost immediately after February 11. Dozens of Mubarak-era ministers and regime-connected businessmen were summoned for questioning and jailed. One of the first to be targeted was Ahmed Ezz, the wealthy oligarch whose name became synonymous with the so-called businessman's cabinet that dominated the government in Mubarak's final decade.

Suddenly it was open season on just about anyone who wielded any degree of power or prestige under the old system. Now, the very relationships and connections that once were the key to an Egyptian businessman's influence had become a scarlet letter, threatening social disgrace and possible incarceration.

The change had personal implications: in 2010, my wife Rola and I were thinking about buying property in Egypt. At one point, we toured a still-under-construction luxury housing complex on the Red Sea shore in the resort town of Ain Sukhna, about ninety minutes southeast of Cairo. The real estate agent told us (in hushed confidential tones) that one of the main investors in the project was Gamal Mubarak's father-in-law. The implication was that with the Mubarak connection in place, the development would never have any troubles with licensing, municipal services, or red tape.

We ended up not buying there for a variety of factors, but one main reason was that we would essentially be gambling that the Mubarak family would remain in control of the country, a risk I wasn't willing to take with our life savings.

Among Cairo's wealthier classes, a deep paranoia took hold; a fear that anyone who prospered in the last two decades would be automatically targeted.

"The problem is, what if Egypt becomes a place where we vilify everyone who did well [under Mubarak]," said one veteran corporate communications specialist who comes from a prominent and powerful family. She agreed to an interview only on condition of anonymity, saying that wealthy families like hers "didn't want to stick out" in postrevolutionary Egypt. "The elite feel that they've gone from the center to the margins," she said. "It's the post-traumatic stress of the elite facing a new reality."

As with any such postrevolutionary process, the trick is knowing when to stop for the sake of the country. If everyone who benefited from or participated in the corruption of the Mubarak regime was to be held accountable, then half the nation would spend the next ten years putting the other half on trial.

"They have to be careful not to push too hard. They can't get everyone who was corrupt or the economy will come down," Hisham Kassem said. "They need to start working a little more towards a truth-and-reconciliation model."

And while nobody was defending the excesses of the Mubarak regime, several prominent Egyptians expressed concern that the postrevolutionary reckoning was taking place haphazardly, with no transparency or apparent pattern. It became impossible to tell just who was being investigated and when the authorities would come knocking.

"Being rich is a crime now," complained Naguib Sawiris, the country's richest businessman and a public proponent of the revolution, in a March 2011 interview with the *Wall Street Journal.*

"It's like a shark feeding frenzy," said a wealthy Egyptian businessman and former member of Mubarak's ruling National Democratic Party. "I'm strongly anti-corruption, but everything must have a due process. Everybody should be innocent until proven guilty and not the other way around. Otherwise everybody freezes in place and worries that they're next."

The businessman, who spoke with me on condition of anonymity, said several of his friends and acquaintances had been arrested. One friend, a wealthy seventy-year-old real estate developer, was taken "at 1 A.M. in his pajamas."

Determined to avoid the same fate, the businessman said he personally sought out prosecutors and asked to see his investigative file.

"I didn't want to wait," he said. "If I had skeletons, I wanted them to come out now."

The economy under Mubarak was structured so that a certain amount of under-the-table kickbacks were simply built into the system and regarded as the price of doing business. Many now complained that a truly unrestrained anticorruption investigation would be like pulling a loose thread on a sweater until the entire garment was in tatters.

"Give me the names of the top 100 companies in Egypt and show me the company that wasn't somehow involved with [the Mubaraks]," said Nathalie Atalla, a marketing executive at one of Egypt's top technology firms. "The witch hunt that we've been seeing has taken a very nasty turn. Anyone who's anyone is starting to get worried."

The need for some sort of mass purge extends well beyond the corridors of Egyptian power and the boardrooms of the elite. Almost every public institution—from university faculties to the prosecutor's office itself—is littered with nepotistic hires and NDP loyalists. One of the more unlikely targets for the postrevolutionary vengeance has been in the realm of the arts. During the revolution, a steady stream of Egyptian actors and musicians took to the airwaves to express their support for Mubarak and sometimes to vilify the Tahrir protesters. In one notorious example, veteran actor Talaat Zakaria went on a lengthy televised rant about how Tahrir was overrun with drugged-out young anarchists having sex in their tents. About five minutes later, without a hint of irony, he described the square as being dominated by the Muslim

Brotherhood. Exactly where the drug-fueled orgy stopped and the Islamic Republic of Tahrir began was never quite made clear. Either way, he earned himself top billing on multiple blacklists drawn up by activists in the wake of the revolution.

Another favorite blacklist target was young heart-throb singer Tamer Hosny—a sort of watered-down Justin Timberlake. Hosny made the mistake of his career midway through the revolution by going on television, referring to Mubarak as "our father" and urging the Tahrir protesters to go home. He was, of course, immediately vilified and savagely caricatured inside the square. Sensing this unexpected backlash, Hosny attempted to fix the damage by visiting revolutionary Tahrir Square; he barely made it out alive and had to be physically evacuated one step ahead of the enraged crowds. A subsequent video of a traumatized Hosny incoherently weeping was gleefully forwarded around the Internet.

The campaign to blackball pro-Mubarak artists has mostly been an entertaining diversion. A far more serious battle is being waged to make sure that prominent NDP members don't sneak back into power via the ballot box. One of the main points of debate between activist groups and the SCAF during the summer of 2011 was how much of the new parliament would be elected via party lists and how much via direct elections. Most activists advocated a heavy dependence on European-style party lists—where citizens would vote for a party rather than an individual and each party would stock the parliament based on the percentage it received. Their reasoning was that individual district elections would automatically favor the incumbent NDP representative, who would retain his local prestige, connections and ill-gotten wealth and would be able to buy his way back into power. The SCAF originally planned to fill the parliament with a fifty/fifty split between the party list and American-style individual electoral systems. But they were forced to change to a two thirds dependence on party lists after a broad coalition of parties—including the Muslim Brotherhood—threatened a blanket boycott.

One of the institutions most resistant to reform has been the one that needs it the most: the Interior Ministry. To the frustration of many, the SCAF has seemingly handled the Interior file with kid gloves. The ground-level police returned meekly to their posts; State Security was renamed National Security and a few prominent generals were shuffled around or put to pasture. But the structure and many of the personalities remain. One of the most pressing challenges of the first elected postrevolutionary government will be to truly force a change in the internal culture of the police state—starting with the installation of a civilian Interior Minister with strong backing and real authority to truly clean the stables.

. "That definitely needs to happen but it needs to come from an elected government with a popular mandate," said Wael Khalil.

Alaa Al Aswany, the author and columnist, describes a massive purge of the Interior Ministry as not merely a preference in building a strong and democratic new Egypt. To him, it's an absolute necessity to ensure that Egypt even makes it through the post-Mubarak transitional period. The failure to immediately reconstitute the security state after Mubarak's departure has, he said, created a thousands-strong armed counterrevolutionary insurgent force inside the Egyptian government.

"Basically every general in State Security is guilty of a crime against the Egyptian people. And they know that once we have a fair election, we're probably going to send them to jail for 20 years," Al Aswany said. "So now, I'm the director of security for Alexandria and I know there's a few months left before the elections. Am I going to do my job sincerely and smooth the path to elections so you can jail me? Of course I'm going to cause trouble and spark problems between Muslims and Christians and set fires here and there and ruin the elections. I'm fighting for my life here."

It was a day many Egyptians never thought would come, even after watching Hosni Mubarak meekly driven from power. If you conducted a poll of Egyptians on February 12, the day after Mubarak was forced to resign, even then the vast majority still probably wouldn't have believed they'd ever see the day when the man who dominated nearly three decades of the country's history would be locked in a courtroom cage facing trial.

The word "unprecedented" is one that's tossed around a little too easily these days. But for once, on August 3, 2011, it was a completely appropriate way to describe what happened in Egypt. Even in the context of the massive upheavals rocking the region, this was uncharted territory. Never in the modern Middle East has a leader been ousted and subsequently tried by his own people. Saddam Hussein was removed by a U.S.-led military invasion, not by Iraqis. And his trial took place in a country under foreign occupation—something which, fairly or not, gives it a permanent stigma in the minds of many Arabs. Tunisia's Zine al-Abidine Ben Ali was tried and sentenced after that country's revolution—but in absentia while he sat safely in exile in Saudi Arabia.

On August 3, normal life in Egypt ground to a halt as everyone seemed transfixed by the nearest television. They watched as Mubarak was transported via helicopter and then ambulance to a specially designed courtroom within a huge lecture hall inside the former Mubarak Police Academy. The eighty-three-year-old—clad in a white prison jumpsuit but still sporting his trademark jet black dye-job—spent the entire session lying on a hospital gurney, occasionally whispering to his sons (and co-defendants) Gamal and Alaa. He seemed drained, frail and broken, although there was healthy speculation that the death-bed routine was an act to provoke sympathy. He spoke publicly only once, to answer the judge on charges of corruption and ordering lethal force against protesters during the revolution.

"I am here, your honor," Mubarak responded into a microphone when the judge called on him. "I categorically deny them all."

The sight was one that sparked widespread disbelief along with spontaneous outbursts of national pride and a healthy dose of malicious glee from some. Despite his two sons' efforts to stand between their father and the television cameras, images of Mubarak apparently picking his nose rocketed around Twitter within minutes. The next day's *Al-Ahram* sported a banner headline that proclaimed, "The Pharaoh Locked in a Cage."

Even in powerless disgrace, Mubarak proved himself able to provoke divisions and to polarize the nation. His first several sessions before the court were marred by violent clashes between pro- and anti-Mubarak protesters outside the police academy. Eventually the presiding judge and the SCAF decided to stop broadcasting the Mubarak trial sessions live; the judge ruled that testimony from key players such as Field Marshal Tantawi would be subject to a blanket media gag order. Understandably, these decisions stoked rumors that the judicial fix was in and that Mubarak would never actually be convicted by the system he personally helped build. The fact that the SCAF was so obviously reluctant to arrest Mubarak— doing so only to appease fresh waves of protests—fueled a belief that Mubarak had been given pre-resignation assurances that he would be free from the legal reckoning.

Tantawi himself seriously muddied those waters. Despite the gag order on his testimony, he publicly declared in a speech that he had never received an order from Mubarak to use live ammunition against protesters.

But aside from the conspiracy theories, there's another factor potentially hindering efforts to bring Mubarak and his deputies to justice: the Egyptian Public Prosecutor's Office might not actually be up to the job. As with any public sector entity, the prosecutor's office is loaded with nepotistic hires and regime cronies; suddenly this same deeply flawed entity was expected to handle dozens of complicated and high-profile investigations—the daunting equivalent of a combined FBI mafia investigation and an international war crimes tribunal. The prosecutor's postrevolutionary track record was spotty at best. Several easy targets like former ministers had been sentenced to jail terms and former Interior Minister al-Adly and his main subordinates had all been convicted of a variety of offenses. But very few police or State Security commanders had been successfully convicted for their actions before and during the revolution. The trial of twenty-five ranking officials and NDP parliamentarians charged with organizing the February 2 assault on Tahrir Square was riddled with prosecutorial missteps and witnesses abruptly reversing their testimony.

The personal fate of Hosni Mubarak matters very deeply to many, many Egyptians, but it actually doesn't matter that much to the nation. Acquitting and releasing him to live out his days in brokenhearted house arrest won't destroy the progress of the revolution; but nor will executing him or jailing him for life guarantee that any of those revolutionary ambitions will be realized. Mubarak's time is finished. The protesters who succeeded in "dragging him from his castle" may soon realize that figuring out what comes next will be much more difficult. Perhaps the best revenge Egyptians can enact against their longtime dictator is having rendered him irrelevant to Egypt's future.

EPILOGUE

The Cairo Effect

If Tunisia led directly to Egypt, then what could Egypt lead to? Egyptians tend to think of themselves as the sun around which the rest of the Middle East revolves, like planets caught in Cairo's gravitational pull. In this case, they might be right.

Egypt, by virtue of its population, history and geographic position, has always held tremendous sway over the region. The 1952 revolution that overthrew the Egyptian monarchy (really more of an extremely popular coup than a true revolution) led directly to a host of similar transitions around the region. But none of the militarized pseudo-republics that replaced the monarchies in Cairo, Tripoli, Baghdad, and elsewhere produced anything resembling a functioning democracy or a just society.

Now, sixty years later, the Egyptian people face another historic opportunity; at stake is far more than just the fate of one country. A properly rebuilt Egypt—one structured around rule of law, firm governmental checks and balances, and trusted, uncorrupted national institutions—could gradually transform the Middle East. An Egypt built around the idea of a true meritocracy, a place where the people can choose their own leaders and then peacefully choose different ones could become the proverbial "light unto the nations" for a region that has been sliding backward for most of the past century.

The idea of establishing Egypt as a meritocracy might be the single most important change going forward—arguably more important than dismantling the security state or even free and fair elections. Put simply, modern Egypt has spent most of the last several decades squandering the abilities and potential of one of the most clever, resourceful, and resilient populations on the planet. Rigid class distinctions, endemic nepotism, and a culture where the sacred god of *wusta* (influence, connections) trumped all else killed the ambitions and work ethic of multiple generations. If your father was a *bowab*, like the Taha character in *The Yacoubian Building*, then it didn't matter how smart or dedicated you were. If you were born anything less than wealthy and connected, there wasn't much point in trying—so eventually people stopped. Those who wanted more for themselves often had to leave the country to find the success that matched their ambitions and skills.

Over the past fifteen years, I've had literally hundreds of conversations with Egyptians who were desperately curious to know what life was like in America. Often I had to shoot down the "streets paved with gold" fantasies of those who thought they would simply be handed a wonderful life upon arrival at JFK Airport. I would point out that very little was easy in the United States and most Americans work far harder and longer than their Egyptian counterparts in any field. But I also had to admit that America, compared to Egypt, really was a land of opportunity. If you were smart, dedicated, and disciplined, you would probably do all right, no matter who your father was.

Recreating Egypt as a land of true economic opportunity could take decades. But it's one of the most pressing challenges facing all post-Mubarak governments. Failure to do so risks a descent into further darkness and unrest that could drag the entire region even further backward.

"If in a couple of years, the person who was sweeping my street and who was just as instrumental as I was in this whole thing, finds that 'Well, things have been good for Hisham, but I'm still sweeping the street and living on $2 a day,' they will rise again," said Hisham Kassem.

Around the region, the Cairo Effect was instantaneous. Parallel revolts sprang up almost immediately in Syria, Libya, Bahrain, and Yemen. But they all proved messier, more complicated, and far bloodier. In Libya and Syria, the countries' militaries openly attacked civilians. In Bahrain there was an even more appalling spectacle. The tiny island nation with a majority Shiite Muslim population is governed by force by a minority Sunni royal family. When the mostly Shiite protesters began to overwhelm the local police force, they quickly learned that they were battling far more than just their own repressive government. Several other neighboring gulf countries immediately sent their own forces in to help crush the peaceful protesters—all while the U.S. government offered only muted criticism of Bahrain, its close ally and home of the Fifth Fleet of the U.S. Navy. It was a sobering lesson—clear proof that realpolitik and a desire for fake and unsustainable stability can still trump the legitimate and peaceful aspirations of an oppressed population.

Other Arab nations have been able to avoid mass unrest by moving proactively. In Morocco, Jordan, and Saudi Arabia, the monarchies suddenly offered long-demanded domestic reforms, in a desperate attempt to avoid the same fate as Mubarak and exiled former president of Tunisia, Zine al-Abidine Ben Ali. None of these would have arisen in the absence of an Arab Spring to finally make the region's leaders take notice—and fear—the will of their peoples.

Then there's Israel, where the government is openly nervous about the loss of its longtime "peace partner" in Cairo. The fact that the country, which has long proclaimed itself "the only democracy in the Middle East," was so clearly unhappy with the potential emergence of a second democracy speaks volumes about just how twisted and backward the politics of the region have become.

Those postrevolutionary fears were massively inflated by the fierce local reaction to an August cross-border shooting incident in the Sinai Peninsula that left several Egyptian border guards dead. Local activists seized the opportunity to focus anew on the Israeli embassy in Giza with a series of dramatic protests that culminated in the Israeli flag being removed from the building and the embassy itself being temporarily overrun by enraged crowds.

When Prime Minister Essam Sharaf casually remarked in an interview that the Camp David treaty "isn't sacred," the Israeli government hit the roof and summoned the Egyptian ambassador for an immediate explanation.

But despite the anxiety in Jerusalem, the fall of Mubarak could end up producing a stronger and more mature Israeli-Egyptian relationship. It may take years, with some bumps in the road, but there's a chance for Camp David to evolve into an actual peace between peoples rather than a mere treaty between governments.

Egyptians may feel a strong antipathy toward Israel and deep sympathy for the Palestinians, but almost nobody wants to return to war. If the Egyptian people were actually offered a choice in the matter, I believe they would vote to remain at peace with Israel—perhaps with some additional provisions that gave Cairo more leeway to alleviate the suffering in the Gaza Strip.

Under Mubarak, the Camp David Accords created a whole host of unhealthy dynamics on both sides of the border. For decades, from the international viewpoint, Mubarak could do whatever he wanted domestically as long as he kept to the Camp David agreement. His status as an invaluable "moderate" among Arab nations was entirely pinned on his ability to force an unpopular position onto his own people.

Meanwhile Israel fell into a dangerous and self-destructive rut—knowing that with Egypt's president on its side, it could essentially ignore public opinion in its largest and most important regional ally. They simply counted on Mubarak to shove the situation down his people's throats. And for years he cleverly managed that popular anger, using it to divert attention away from domestic concerns. As long as Egyptians were busy burning Israeli flags, they weren't thinking about burning down the local police station or the National Democratic Party headquarters. The moment, around 2003, when domestic grievances began taking precedence over foreign policy issues was the beginning of the end for Mubarak's reign.

Now, for the first time in decades, the opinion of the Egyptian people will be heard. That's undeniably a good thing for Egypt. But it might just end up creating a healthier environment for Israel and the rest of the Middle East in the process.

INDEX

INDEX

INDEX

ML   1-12